Southern [

Main Dishes, Salads, Sides & More!

S. L. Watson

DEDICATION

To everyone who has ever had their garden grow too many tomatoes!

CONTENTS

INTRODUCTION

There is nothing I enjoy more in a southern garden than fresh ripe tomatoes. We long all year for the fresh and natural taste of vine ripened tomatoes. Ripe, juicy and so good with most any meal. During the summer, tomatoes are eaten at most every meal in my house.

In the summer, it seems I always grow more tomatoes than we can eat. I am always looking for new ideas to use the tomatoes. Included are southern favorites for using your home grown tomatoes year round. Recipes include Grilled Cilantro Lime Griddle Cake Sandwiches, Stuffed Green Tomato Casserole, Fresh Tomato Chunky Marinara Sauce, Raspberry Tomato Jam, Rustic Spinach and Tomato Tart, Fried Green Tomato Salad and Tomato Parmesan Gnocchi. Enjoy fresh salads, southern sides, savory pies, tarts, main dishes and more with this southern recipe collection.

1 APPETIZERS, SAUCES & SPREADS

Tomatoes are known for the most famous sauce and appetizers. We all love marinara sauce and bruschetta is at the top of everyone's list. Tomatoes are great for crostinis, sauces, dips and spreads. Tomatoes are an easy way to add fresh ingredients to your appetizers.

Smoked Salmon Tomato Cups

Makes 2 dozen

24 cherry tomatoes
3 oz. pkg. smoked cooked salmon, finely chopped
1/4 cup cottage cheese
2 tbs. finely chopped celery
1 tbs. finely chopped green onion
1/4 tsp. dried dill

Cut a thin slice off the top of each tomato. Scoop out the pulp and discard. Place the tomatoes, upside down, on paper towels. Let the tomatoes drain for 30 minutes.

In a small bowl, add the salmon, cottage cheese, celery, green onion and dill. Stir until combined. Place the tomatoes in a serving dish. Spoon the salmon into the tomatoes. Chill for 2 hours before serving.

Tomato Chutney Cheesecake

Makes 18 appetizer servings

32 oz. cream cheese, softened
2 cups shredded cheddar cheese
1/2 tsp. cayenne pepper
5 green onions, finely chopped
2/3 cup red tomato chutney
2 tbs. whole milk
Assorted raw vegetables and crackers

In a mixing bowl, add 24 ounces cream cheese, cheddar cheese and cayenne pepper. Using a mixer on medium speed, beat until smooth and creamy. Turn the mixer off and stir in the green onions.

Line an 8" round cake pan with plastic wrap. Spread half the cream cheese mixture in the cake pan. Spread the tomato chutney over the cream cheese. Spread the remaining cream cheese mixture over the chutney. Cover the cheesecake with plastic wrap and refrigerate for 24 hours.

Invert the cheesecake on a serving platter. Remove the plastic wrap. In a mixing bowl, add 1 tablespoon milk and 8 ounces cream cheese. Stir until smooth and combined. Spread over the top and sides of the cheesecake like frosting. If the cream cheese is not creamy, add the remaining tablespoon milk. Serve with raw vegetables and crackers.

Marinated Cherry Tomatoes

Makes 8 servings

4 cups cherry tomatoes
1/2 cup vodka
1 tsp. salt
8 oz. goat cheese log

Poke the stem end of each cherry tomato with a toothpick. Add the tomatoes to a mixing bowl with a lid. Pour the vodka over the tomatoes. Sprinkle the salt over the tomatoes. Place a lid on the bowl and shake until the tomatoes are coated in the vodka. Refrigerate the tomatoes for 3 hours.

Remove the tomatoes from the bowl and place on a serving platter. Place slices of the goat cheese around the tomatoes and serve.

Caprese Cheese Sticks

This appetizer is so easy to prepare. Great snack for ball games.

Makes 6 appetizer servings

1 tbs. olive oil
1 tbs. balsamic vinegar
1 garlic clove, minced
1/4 tsp. salt
1/4 tsp. black pepper
2 cups cherry tomatoes
18 frozen cheese sticks
2 tbs. minced fresh basil

Preheat the oven to 400°. Place the cheese sticks on a baking sheet. In a mixing bowl, add the olive oil, balsamic vinegar, garlic, salt and black pepper. Stir until well combined. Add the tomatoes and toss until the tomatoes are coated in the marinade. Spread the tomatoes on a separate baking pan.

Bake the tomatoes and cheese sticks for 15 minutes or until the cheese sticks are golden brown. Remove the tomatoes and cheese sticks from the oven. Place the cheese sticks on a serving platter. Spoon the tomatoes over the top of the cheese sticks. Sprinkle the basil over the top and serve.

Fresh Garden Salsa

Makes 5 cups

6 tomatoes, finely chopped
3/4 cup finely chopped green bell pepper
1/2 cup finely chopped onion
1/2 cup thinly sliced green onion
6 garlic cloves, minced
2 tsp. cider vinegar
2 tsp. fresh lemon juice
2 tsp. vegetable oil
2 tsp. minced jalapeno pepper
2 tsp. ground cumin
1/2 tsp. salt
1/4 tsp. cayenne pepper

Add all the ingredients to a large bowl. Stir until well combined. Cover the bowl and refrigerate for 2 hours before serving.

Fresh Tomato Peach Salsa

Makes 5 cups

3 cups seeded and diced tomatoes
1 avocado, peeled, pitted and diced
1/2 cup diced green bell pepper
2 cups peeled and diced fresh peaches
1/2 cup chopped green onion
1/3 cup chopped fresh cilantro
1 1/2 tsp. balsamic vinegar
1/2 tsp. season salt

Add all the ingredients to a serving bowl. Toss until all the ingredients are combined. Serve the salsa at room temperature.

Peach Green Tomato Salsa

Makes 6 cups

This is so good with chicken, pork or fish.

4 green tomatoes, chopped
2 large peaches, chopped
6 sliced green onions
1/2 cup olive oil
1/4 cup white wine vinegar
2 tbs. minced fresh cilantro
2 tbs. lemon juice
1 tbs. vinegar from bottled hot peppers
1 tbs. honey
1 tsp. salt

Add all the ingredients to a mixing bowl. Stir until all the ingredients are combined. Cover the bowl and chill for 1 hour before serving.

Garden Bruschetta

Makes 14 servings

1 garlic clove, peeled and halved
14 French bread slices, 3/4" thick
4 tomatoes, seeded and diced
1/4 cup chopped purple onion
2 tbs. olive oil
1 tbs. minced fresh basil
1/4 tsp. salt
1/8 tsp. black pepper
14 fresh basil leaves

Rub one side of each French bread slice with the garlic halves. Preheat the oven to 350°. Place the bread slices, garlic side down, on a baking sheet. Bake for 5 minutes on each side or until the bread is lightly toasted. Remove the bread from the oven.

In a mixing bowl, add the tomatoes, purple onion, olive oil, minced basil, salt and black pepper. Toss until all the ingredients are combined. Place the toasted bread slices on a serving platter. Spoon 2 tablespoons tomato topping on each bread slice. Place a fresh basil leaf on each slice and serve.

Tomato, Caper and Olive Bruschetta

Makes 18 appetizers

3 cups diced fresh tomato
1/2 tsp. salt
1/2 tsp. diced kalamata olives
3 garlic cloves, minced
2 tbs. olive oil
2 tbs. balsamic vinegar
3 tbs. capers, drained
2 tbs. chopped fresh basil
1 tsp. granulated sugar
1/2 tsp. black pepper
18 toasted French baguette slices

In a mixing bowl, add the tomatoes, salt, olives, garlic, olive oil, balsamic vinegar, capers, basil, granulated sugar and black pepper. Stir until all the ingredients are combined. Cover the bowl and chill for 1 hour.

Drain any liquid from the tomatoes. Spoon the mixture onto the baguette slices and serve.

Garlic Tomato Crostini

Makes 2 dozen

24 French bread slices, 1/4" thick
1/4 cup olive oil
1/2 tsp. garlic powder
6 mozzarella cheese slices, 1 oz. each
1 1/2 cups chopped and seeded tomatoes

Turn the oven to the broiler position. Place the bread slices on a baking sheet. In a small bowl, add the olive oil and garlic powder. Stir until combined and brush on the bread slices. Cut each mozzarella cheese slice into 4 pieces. Place a mozzarella cheese piece on each bread slice. Broil the crostini for 3 minutes or until the cheese is melted and the bread toasted.

Remove the pan from the oven and sprinkle the tomatoes over the top. Serve hot.

Tomato Cheese Bread

Makes 6 servings

8 oz. cream cheese, softened
1/4 cup shredded Parmesan cheese
1 garlic clove, minced
2 tbs. chopped fresh basil
1/4 tsp. salt
1/8 tsp. black pepper
16 oz. loaf French bread
2 fresh tomatoes, sliced

In a mixing bowl, add the cream cheese, Parmesan cheese, garlic, basil, salt and black pepper. Stir until combined. Cut the French bread in half horizontally. Spread the cream cheese mixture over the cut side of each bread half.

Preheat the oven to the broiler position. Place the bread halves, topping side up, on a baking sheet. Place the tomatoes over the cream cheese mixture. Broil for 5 minutes or until the topping is bubbly and the cheese melted. Remove the bread from the oven and cut into slices. Serve the bread hot.

Tomato Goat Cheese Crostini

Makes 20 appetizers

2 large tomatoes, seeded and diced
1/8 tsp. salt
2 tbs. plus 1 tsp. olive oil
6 oz. herb flavored goat cheese, crumbled
2 tbs. chopped fresh basil
1/4 tsp. black pepper
20 French baguette slices, 1/2" thick
2 garlic cloves, peeled and halved
2 tsp. chopped fresh parsley

In a mixing bowl, add the tomatoes, salt and 1 teaspoon olive oil. Toss until all the ingredients are combined. In a small bowl, add the goat cheese, basil and black pepper. Stir until all the ingredients are combined.

Preheat the oven to 350°. Brush 2 tablespoons olive oil over the baguette slices. Place the baguette slices on a baking sheet. Bake for 6 minutes or until the baguette slices are toasted. Remove the bread from the oven. Immediately rub the garlic cloves over the bread slices.

Spread the goat cheese mixture over one side of the baguette slices. Spoon the tomatoes over the top of the crostini. Sprinkle the parsley over the top and serve.

Spanish Salsa Crostini

Makes 32 appetizers

32 French bread slices, 1/4" thick
1 cup finely chopped mushrooms
1 tbs. chopped fresh parsley
1 tbs. balsamic vinegar
2 tsp. dried basil
1/4 tsp. salt
3 cups fresh diced tomatoes
2 green onions, sliced
6 oz. jar marinated artichokes, drained and finely chopped
1 cup sliced black olives

In a mixing bowl, add the mushrooms, parsley, balsamic vinegar, basil, salt, tomatoes, green onions, artichokes and black olives. Stir until combined. Let the salsa sit for 20 minutes at room temperature.

Preheat the oven to 400°. Place the bread slices on two baking sheets. Bake for 6 minutes or until the bread is lightly toasted. Remove the bread from the oven and place on a serving platter. Spoon the salsa over the bread slices and serve.

Tomato Salad Bruschetta

Makes 12 appetizers

12 French bread slices, 1/2" thick
2 tbs. olive oil
1 garlic clove, minced
1 cup diced tomato
2 tbs. sliced black olives
2 tbs. diced red bell pepper
2 green onions, sliced
1 tbs. Italian dressing
4 fresh basil leaves, sliced
1/4 cup shredded Parmesan cheese

Preheat the oven to 375°. Place the French bread slices on a baking sheet. In a small bowl, add the olive oil and garlic. Stir until combined and brush on the top of the bread slices. Bake for 10 minutes or until the bread slices are toasted and lightly browned. Remove the bread slices from the oven.

In a mixing bowl, add the tomato, black olives, red bell pepper, green onions and Italian dressing. Toss until all the ingredients are combined. Place the bread slices on a serving platter. Spoon the tomato salad over the bread slices. Sprinkle the basil and Parmesan cheese over the top and serve.

Tomato Basil Bruschetta

Makes 16 appetizers

2 cups finely chopped tomatoes
2 tbs. chopped fresh basil
1 tbs. olive oil
1 garlic clove, minced
16 toasted baguette slices, 1/2" thick

In a small bowl, add the tomatoes, basil, olive oil and garlic. Toss until all the ingredients are combined. Let the tomatoes sit for 15 minutes at room temperature.

Place the baguette slices on a serving platter. Spoon the tomatoes on the bread slices and serve.

Tomato Basil Caprese Kabobs

Makes 34 appetizer kabobs

1/4 cup olive oil
2 tbs. lemon juice
2/3 cup freshly chopped basil
1/4 tsp. salt
1/4 tsp. black pepper
1 pint red cherry tomatoes
1 pint yellow cherry tomatoes
2 yellow squash, cubed
1 lb. fresh mozzarella cheese, cubed
34 bamboo skewers, 6" size

In a mixing bowl, add the olive oil, lemon juice, basil, salt and black pepper. Stir until combined. Add the red cherry tomatoes, yellow cherry tomatoes and squash. Toss until combined. Cover the bowl and refrigerate for 30 minutes.

Thread the tomatoes, squash and mozzarella cheese on the skewers. Place the skewers on a serving platter. Drizzle any remaining marinade over the skewers and serve.

Smoky Hot Sauce

Makes 3 cups

1 1/2 cups chopped onion
1 tbs. olive oil
4 garlic cloves, minced
5 cups chopped tomato
3/4 cup water
1 chicken bouillon cube
1 canned chipotle pepper in adobo sauce
2 tbs. adobe sauce from canned chipotle
1 tsp. Tabasco sauce
1/4 tsp. salt

In a dutch oven over medium heat, add the onion and olive oil. Saute the onion for 8 minutes. Add the garlic and saute the garlic for 1 minute. Add the tomatoes, water, chicken bouillon cube, chipotle pepper, adobo sauce, Tabasco sauce and salt to the pan. Stir until all the ingredients are combined.

Bring the sauce to a boil and reduce the heat to low. Stir occasionally and simmer the sauce for 25 minutes. Remove the pan from the heat and cool for 30 minutes.

Spoon the sauce into a blender or food processor. Process until the sauce is smooth. Pour the sauce into a bowl and chill for 8 hours before serving. Use as a basting sauce for meats or serve with chips.

Fresh Tomato Chunky Marinara Sauce

Makes 2 cups

4 garlic cloves, minced
4 tbs. olive oil
3 tbs. tomato paste
4 cups diced fresh tomatoes
2 tbs. fresh lemon juice
4 tbs. chopped fresh basil
Salt and black pepper to taste

In a skillet over medium heat, add the olive oil. When the oil is hot, add the garlic. Saute the garlic for 1 minute. Add the tomato paste to the skillet. Stir constantly and cook for 1 minute. Add the tomatoes and lemon juice to the skillet. Stir frequently and cook for 10 minutes. Remove the skillet from the heat.

Using a potato masher, mash the tomatoes until small chunks remain. Stir in the basil and season with salt and black pepper to taste. Serve hot over pasta, with pizza, cheese sticks or breadsticks.

Tomato and Crabmeat Gravy

This is delicious over grits, rice or biscuits.

Makes 6 servings

4 tbs. unsalted butter
1/4 cup diced onion
3 tbs. all purpose flour
1 1/2 cups chicken broth
1 cup whipping cream
1/2 tsp. salt
1/2 tsp. cayenne pepper
8 oz. fresh lump crabmeat
2 cups diced tomatoes

In a sauce pan over medium heat, add the butter. When the butter melts, add the onion. Saute the onion for 1 minute. Add the all purpose flour to the pan. Stir constantly and cook for 2 minutes. Do not let the flour brown for this gravy.

Whisk in the chicken broth and whipping cream. Whisk until smooth and combined. Add the salt and cayenne pepper to the pan. Whisk until smooth and combined. Bring the gravy to a boil and reduce the heat to low. Stir constantly and simmer until the gravy thickens and bubbles.

Stir in the crabmeat and tomatoes. Cook only until the crab and tomatoes are heated. Remove the pan from the heat and serve.

Raspberry Tomato Jam

This jam sounds unusual but it is very good. Great way to use green tomatoes.

Makes 7 cups

5 1/2 cups chopped green tomatoes
5 1/2 cups granulated sugar
6 oz. pkg. raspberry jello

In a stock pot over medium heat, add the tomatoes and granulated sugar. Stir constantly and bring the tomatoes to a boil. When the tomatoes are boiling, reduce the heat to low. Stir occasionally and simmer the jam for 25 minutes.

Remove the pan from the heat and stir in the jello. Stir for 1 minute or until the jello dissolves. Pour the jam into glass jars. Cool the jam completely at room temperature. Place the lid on the jars and refrigerate up to 3 weeks. Stir the jam before serving to combine the ingredients.

Two Tomato Tapenade

Makes 2 cups

1 1/2 cups fresh tomato, seeded and chopped
12 sun dried tomatoes in oil, drained and chopped
1 cup shredded Italian cheese blend
1/3 cup crumbled Gorgonzola cheese
1/4 cup onion, minced
1 tbs. minced fresh basil
1 tsp. minced fresh rosemary
1/4 tsp. garlic pepper

Add all the ingredients to a mixing bowl. Stir until combined. Serve on crackers, toasted baguette slices or pita rounds.

Tomato Basil Corn Relish

Makes 3 1/2 cups

1/4 cup whole kernel corn
1 teaspoon diced canned green chiles
1 1/2 cups diced tomatoes
1/3 cup chopped purple onion
1/4 cup chopped green bell pepper
2 tbs. chopped fresh basil
1 tbs. chopped fresh cilantro
1 1/2 tbs. red wine vinegar
1 tbs. olive oil
Salt and black pepper to taste

Add the corn, green chiles, tomatoes, purple onion, green bell pepper, basil, cilantro, red wine vinegar and olive oil to a mixing bowl. Toss until all the ingredients are combined. Season to taste with salt and black pepper.

Serve over most any meat, peas or beans. Also great with corn or tortilla chips.

Bacon Tomato Dip

Makes 1 3/4 cups

8 slices bacon, cooked and crumbled
1 tomato, peeled and chopped
8 oz. cream cheese, cubed
1/4 cup mayonnaise
1/4 tsp. salt
1/4 tsp. black pepper
1/4 tsp. dried basil

Add the cream cheese, mayonnaise, salt, black pepper and basil to a food processor. Process until smooth. Spoon into a serving bowl and stir in the bacon and tomato. Chill for 1 hour before serving. Serve with toasted baguette slices, crackers or chips.

Tomato Nacho Dip

Makes 3 cups

4 oz. can chopped green chiles
1/2 cup chopped onion
2 tbs. unsalted butter
2 tbs. all purpose flour
1/2 cup whole milk
1 1/2 cups cubed Velveeta cheese
1 cup shredded Monterey Jack cheese
1 cup chopped fresh tomato

In a sauce pan over medium heat, add the green chiles with any liquid, onion and butter. Saute the green chiles and onion for 5 minutes. Sprinkle the all purpose flour over the chiles and onion. Stir constantly and cook for 2 minutes.

Reduce the heat to low. Add the milk, Velveeta cheese, Monterey Jack cheese and tomato. Stir constantly and cook until the cheeses melt and the dip thickens. Remove the pan from the heat. Spoon the dip into a serving bowl. Serve with tortilla chips or crackers.

Tomato Spinach Dip

Makes 4 cups

8 oz. cream cheese, softened
1/3 cup whole milk
1/4 tsp. salt
1/4 tsp. cayenne pepper
2 tomatoes, seeded and chopped
10 oz. pkg. frozen spinach, thawed

Drain all the liquid from the spinach. Pat the spinach dry with paper towels if needed. In a mixing bowl, add the cream cheese, milk, salt and cayenne pepper. Using a mixer on medium speed, beat until smooth and creamy. Turn the mixer off and stir in the tomatoes and spinach.

Spoon the dip into a microwavable 9" glass pie pan. Microwave for 5 minutes. Remove the dip from the microwave and stir until blended. Serve with crackers, tortilla chips or pita chips.

Fresh Tomato Vegetable Juice

Makes 2 quarts

10 cups chopped fresh tomato
1/2 cup water
1/4 cup chopped green bell pepper
1/4 cup chopped carrot
1/4 cup chopped celery
1/4 cup fresh lemon juice
2 tbs. chopped onion
1 tbs. salt
1 small serrano pepper, seeded and diced

In a stock pot over medium heat, add all the ingredients. Stir until well combined and bring the juice to a boil. When the juice is boiling, reduce the heat to low. Place a lid on the pan and simmer the juice for 30 minutes. Remove the pan from the heat and cool the juice completely.

Unless you have a large blender, you will have to puree the juice in batches. Add the juice to a blender and puree until smooth. Pour into a pitcher and chill before serving.

You do not have to cook the juice if wanting raw juice. Process in a blender as directed above. I prefer the cooked juice as the acidity level is decreased.

Tomato Chutney

Serve over fried green tomatoes, beans or peas.

Makes 5 cups

4 cups diced tomatoes
1 cup light brown sugar
1/2 cup granulated sugar
1 cup diced green bell pepper
1 cup diced onion
2 tbs. ketchup
1 tsp. black pepper
1/4 tsp. Tabasco sauce

Add all the ingredients to a sauce pan over medium heat. Stir until combined and bring the chutney to a boil. When the chutney is boiling, reduce the heat to low. Stir occasionally and cook for 1 1/2 hours or until the chutney thickens. Remove the pan from the heat and serve.

2 MAIN DISHES & CASSEROLES

Tomato pies, tarts and quiche are the most popular ways to use tomatoes in main dishes. They make a great lunch, breakfast or light dinner. Picky eaters tend to eat ripe tomatoes. Use the main dishes to sneak extra nutrition into your diet.

Tomato Onion Pie

Makes 6 servings

8 cups thinly sliced onion
2 tbs. unsalted butter
12 bacon slices, cooked until crisp
2 cups soft breadcrumbs
4 tomatoes, thinly sliced
2 cups shredded cheddar cheese
3 eggs
1/4 tsp. salt
1/8 tsp. black pepper

In a large skillet over medium heat, add the onion slices and butter. Saute the onions for 10 minutes or until they are tender. Remove the skillet from the heat. Crumble 9 bacon slices into a small bowl.

Spray a 9" deep dish pie pan with non stick cooking spray. Spread the breadcrumbs in the bottom of the pie pan. Place half the tomatoes, half the onion, half the crumbled bacon and 1 cup cheddar cheese over the breadcrumbs. Repeat the layering process one more time.

In a mixing bowl, add the eggs, salt and black pepper. Whisk until well combined and pour over the vegetables in the pie crust. Sprinkle 1 cup cheddar cheese over the top. Place the 3 remaining bacon slices over the top of the pie.

Preheat the oven to 350°. Bake for 35 minutes or until a toothpick inserted in the center of the pie comes out clean. Remove the pie from the oven and cool for 5 minutes before serving.

Tomato Bacon Pie

Makes 6 servings

Frozen 9" deep dish pie crust
3 tomatoes, cut into 1/4" slices
10 bacon slices, cooked and crumbled
1 cup shredded cheddar cheese
1 cup mayonnaise

Preheat the oven to 350°. Bake the pie crust for 12 minutes or until the pie crust is lightly browned. Remove the pie crust from the oven and cool completely before filling.

Place the tomatoes in the pie crust. Sprinkle the bacon over the tomatoes. In a small bowl, add the cheddar cheese and mayonnaise. Stir until combined and spread over the top of the pie.

Set the oven temperature to 350°. Bake for 30 minutes or until the pie crust is golden brown and the topping bubbly. Remove the pie from the oven and cool for 5 minutes before slicing.

Beefy Tomato Pie

Makes 6 servings

1 lb. ground beef
1 cup chopped onion
2 tbs. ketchup
1/2 tsp. salt
2 cups Bisquick
2/3 cup whole milk
1 1/2 cups diced fresh tomatoes
1/2 cup shredded cheddar cheese

In a skillet over medium heat, add the ground beef and onion. Stir the ground beef frequently to break the meat into crumbles as it cooks. Cook for 6 minutes or until the ground beef is well browned and no longer pink. Remove the skillet from the heat and drain all the grease from the ground beef. Stir in the ketchup and salt.

In a mixing bowl, add the Bisquick and milk. Stir only until a soft dough forms. Lightly flour your work surface. Place the dough on your surface and knead for 2 minutes. Spray a 10" pie plate with non stick cooking spray. Roll the dough into a 11" circle. Place the dough in the pie plate. Trim and crimp the edges as desired.

Spoon the ground beef filling into the pie crust. Sprinkle the tomatoes over the ground beef. Sprinkle the cheddar cheese over the top of the pie. Preheat the oven to 425°. Bake for 25 minutes or until the crust is done and golden brown. Remove the pie from the oven and serve.

Tomato Quiche

Makes 6 servings

3/4 cup plus 2 tbs. all purpose flour
1/2 cup plain white cornmeal
1 1/2 tsp. salt
1/4 tsp. black pepper
1/3 cup vegetable shortening
5 tbs. ice cold water
2 cups fresh tomatoes, seeded and chopped
1/2 tsp. dried basil
1/2 cup chopped green onion
1/2 cup shredded cheddar cheese
1/2 cup shredded Swiss cheese
2 eggs
1 cup whole milk

In a mixing bowl, add 3/4 cup all purpose flour, cornmeal, 1/2 teaspoon salt and 1/8 teaspoon black pepper. Stir until well combined and add the vegetable shortening to the bowl. Using a pastry blender, cut the shortening into the dry ingredients until you have coarse crumbles. Add 4 tablespoons water to the bowl. Stir with a fork until the dough forms and begins to leave the side of the bowl. Add the remaining tablespoon water if needed to make a soft but firm dough. Wrap the dough in plastic wrap and refrigerate the dough for 30 minutes.

Lightly flour your work surface. Remove the dough from the refrigerator. Roll the dough to a 11" circle. Place the dough in a 9" pie pan. Trim and crimp the edges as desired. Preheat the oven to 375°. Lightly prick the pie crust with a fork. Bake for 10 minutes. Remove the crust from the oven and cool completely before filling.

Place the tomatoes in the bottom of the cooled pie crust. Sprinkle 1 teaspoon salt, basil, 1/8 teaspoon black pepper, green onion, cheddar cheese and Swiss cheese over the tomatoes.

In a mixing bowl, add 2 tablespoons all purpose flour, eggs and milk. Whisk until combined and pour over the filling in the pie crust. Preheat the oven to 375°. Bake for 40 minutes or until a knife inserted off center of the quiche comes out clean. Remove the quiche from the oven and cool for 10 minutes before serving.

Tomato Spinach Quiche

Makes 6 servings

10 oz. pkg. frozen chopped spinach, thawed
2 cups diced tomatoes
2 tbs. Italian seasoned breadcrumbs
3 eggs, beaten
1 cup half and half
4 bacon slices, cooked and crumbled
1/2 cup shredded sharp cheddar cheese
1/2 cup shredded mozzarella cheese
1 tsp. dried basil
1/4 tsp. cayenne pepper
9" deep dish frozen pie crust, unbaked

Drain all the liquid from the spinach. Squeeze the spinach dry with paper towels. In a small bowl, add the tomatoes and breadcrumbs. Toss until the tomatoes are coated in the breadcrumbs.

In a mixing bowl, add the spinach, eggs, half and half, bacon, cheddar cheese, mozzarella cheese, basil and cayenne pepper. Whisk until well blended. Gently fold in the tomatoes. Pour the filling into the pie crust.

Preheat the oven to 350°. Bake for 50 minutes or until a toothpick inserted in the center of the quiche comes out clean. Remove the quiche from the oven and cool for 10 minutes before serving.

Tomato & Cheese Omelet

Makes 4 servings

4 eggs
4 egg whites
4 tbs. water
2 tbs. finely chopped cilantro
1/2 tsp. salt
1/4 tsp. black pepper
1 tbs. unsalted butter
1/2 cup shredded cheddar cheese
1 1/4 cups diced tomato

In a mixing bowl, add the eggs, egg whites, water, cilantro, salt and black pepper. Whisk until well combined. In a 12" skillet over medium heat, add the butter. When the butter melts, pour the eggs into the skillet.

Let the eggs cook for 2 minutes or until the edges of the omelet are set. Using a spatula, carefully lift the edges of the omelet to allow the uncooked eggs to flow underneath. Cook for 4 minutes or until the eggs are almost set. Sprinkle the cheddar cheese over the top of the omelet.

Place a lid on the skillet and cook for 1 minute or until the omelet is set and the cheese melted. Spoon the tomatoes on half of the omelet. Flip the other half of the omelet over the tomatoes. Remove the skillet from the heat. Carefully slide the omelet onto a platter and serve.

Rustic Tomato Tart

Makes 8 servings

12 sheets frozen phyllo dough, thawed
2 tbs. olive oil
2 tbs. dry breadcrumbs
2 tbs. pesto
3/4 cup crumbled feta cheese
2 large tomatoes, cut into 1/4" slices
1/4 tsp. black pepper
5 basil leaves, thinly sliced

Line a baking sheet with parchment paper. Place one phyllo sheet on the parchment paper. Spread 1/2 teaspoon olive oil over the phyllo sheet. Brush the oil all the way to the edges. Sprinkle 1/2 teaspoon breadcrumbs over the phyllo sheet. Repeat until all the phyllo sheets, olive oil and breadcrumbs are used. The phyllo sheets will be stacked on top of each other to form a crust.

Fold each side of the phyllo sheets in about 1" to form a rim. Preheat the oven to 400°. Spread the pesto over the top of the crust. Sprinkle half the feta cheese over the pesto sauce. Place the tomato slices over the crust. Sprinkle the black pepper over the tomatoes. Sprinkle the remaining feta cheese over the tomatoes.

Bake for 20 minutes or until the crust is crispy and golden brown. Remove the tart from the oven and sprinkle the basil over the tart. Cool for 5 minutes before serving.

Tuscan Spinach & Tomato Tart

Makes 4 servings

9" refrigerated pie crust
6 oz. cream cheese, softened
5 tsp. basil pesto
10 oz. pkg. frozen spinach, thawed
1/3 cup diced purple onion
2 cups thinly sliced tomatoes
2 tbs. roasted sunflower seeds
1/2 cup shredded provolone cheese
2 fresh basil leaves, shredded

Preheat the oven to 375°. Spray a 12" pizza pan with non stick cooking spray. Place the pie crust in the pan. Spread the pie crust all the way to the edges of the pan. The crust should resemble a pizza crust. In a small bowl, add the cream cheese and basil pesto. Stir until combined and spread over the top of the pie crust.

Pat the spinach dry with paper towels. Spread the spinach over the pie crust. Place the purple onion, tomatoes, sunflower seeds and provolone cheese over the pie crust. Bake for 30 minutes or until the crust is golden brown. Remove the tart from the oven and sprinkle the basil leaves over the top before serving.

Tomato Vegetable Gratin

Makes 6 servings

2 garlic cloves, minced
3 fresh tomatoes, cut into 1/4" slices
3 red potatoes, cut into 1/8" slices
1/2 cup thinly sliced purple onion
7 oz. jar roasted red bell peppers, drained and chopped
2 cups thinly sliced zucchini
1 cup sliced fresh mushrooms
3/4 tsp. salt
3/4 tsp. black pepper
3 tbs. olive oil
1/2 cup finely crumbled leftover cornbread
1 tbs. Dijon mustard
1/4 cup grated Parmesan cheese
2 tbs. dried Italian seasoning

Spray a 11 x 7 baking dish with non stick cooking spray. Sprinkle the garlic over the baking dish. Layer the tomatoes in the dish. Sprinkle 1/8 teaspoon salt and 1/8 teaspoon black pepper over the tomatoes. Layer the potatoes over the tomatoes. Sprinkle 1/8 teaspoon salt and 1/8 teaspoon black pepper over the potatoes. Layer the onion over the potatoes. Sprinkle 1/8 teaspoon salt and 1/8 teaspoon black pepper over the onion. Layer the roasted red bell peppers over the onion. Sprinkle 1/8 teaspoon salt and 1/8 teaspoon black pepper over the red bell peppers. Layer the zucchini over the red bell peppers. Sprinkle 1/8 teaspoon salt and 1/8 teaspoon black pepper over the zucchini. Layer the mushrooms over the zucchini. Sprinkle 1/8 teaspoon salt and 1/8 teaspoon black pepper over the mushrooms.

Drizzle 2 tablespoons olive oil over the top of the vegetables. Preheat the oven to 350°. Bake for 45 minutes. In a small bowl, add the cornbread, 1 tablespoon olive oil, Dijon mustard, Parmesan cheese and Italian seasoning. Stir until combined and sprinkle over the top of the dish. Bake for 10 minutes or until the cornbread is golden brown. Remove the dish from the oven and cool for 10 minutes before serving.

BLT Tomato Basil Tart

Makes 6 servings

9" refrigerated pie crust, at room temperature
1/3 cup crushed butter crackers
3/4 cup grated Parmesan cheese
3/4 cup mayonnaise
2 cups sliced tomatoes, 1/4" thick
1/2 tsp. salt
1/2 tsp. black pepper
1/4 cup finely shredded fresh basil
12 slices bacon, cooked and crumbled

Preheat the oven to 350°. Place the pie crust in a 9" tart pan. Using a fork, lightly prick the pie crust. You do not want the pie crust to puff up while baking. Bake for 12 minutes or until the pie crust is lightly browned. Remove the crust from the oven but leave the oven on.

Sprinkle the butter crackers over the pie crust. In a small bowl, add the Parmesan cheese and mayonnaise. Stir until combined and spread half the mixture over the bottom and sides of the pie crust. Layer the tomato slices in the pie crust. Sprinkle the salt, black pepper, basil and bacon over the tomatoes. Spread the remaining mayonnaise mixture over the top.

Bake for 25 minutes or until the tart is golden brown. Remove the tart from the oven and cool for 5 minutes before serving.

Fontina Tomato Tart

Makes 4 servings

9" refrigerated pie crust
1 garlic bulb
1/2 tsp. olive oil
1 1/2 cups shredded fontina cheese
4 large tomatoes, cut into 1/4" slices
1/2 tsp. salt
1/4 tsp. black pepper

Preheat the oven to 425°. Place the pie crust in the bottom and sides of a 9" tart pan. Bake for 9 minutes or until the pie crust is lightly browned. Remove the pie crust from the oven but leave the oven on. Cool the crust completely before filling.

Cut off the pointed end of the garlic bulb. Place the garlic on a sheet of aluminum foil. Place the foil on a baking sheet. Drizzle the olive oil over the garlic. Wrap the aluminum foil around the garlic. Bake for 30 minutes. Remove the garlic from the oven. Squeeze the garlic from the bulb into the baked pie crust. Spread the garlic on the bottom of the pie crust.

Sprinkle the tomatoes with salt and black pepper. Place the tomatoes on paper towels and allow them to sit for 10 minutes. Sprinkle 1/2 cup Fontina cheese over the garlic in the pie crust. Place the tomatoes over the cheese. Sprinkle 1 cup Fontina cheese over the tomatoes. Preheat the oven to 350°. Bake for 45 minutes or until the pie crust is golden brown. Remove the tart from the oven and cool for 5 minutes before serving.

Tomato Leek & Bacon Tart

Makes 4 servings

9" refrigerated pie crust
2 cups shredded Italian cheese blend
1 cup sliced leeks
2 tbs. olive oil
4 tomatoes, thinly sliced
1 cup chopped fresh basil
3 garlic cloves, minced
8 bacon slices, cooked and chopped
1/2 cup mayonnaise
1/4 cup freshly grated Parmesan cheese
1 tbs. fresh lemon juice
1/2 tsp. black pepper

Preheat the oven to 450°. Place the pie crust in the bottom and sides of a 9" tart pan. Bake for 10 minutes or until the crust is lightly browned. Leave the oven on but reduce the heat to 375°. Remove the crust from the oven and sprinkle 1 cup Italian cheese blend over the pie crust. Place the tomato slices over the cheese.

In a skillet over medium heat, add the olive oil. When the oil is hot, add the leeks. Saute the leeks for 5 minutes or until they are tender. Remove the skillet from the heat and spoon the leeks over the tomatoes. Sprinkle the basil and garlic over the leeks and tomatoes.

In a mixing bowl, add 1 cup Italian cheese blend, bacon, mayonnaise, Parmesan cheese, lemon juice and black pepper. Whisk until well combined and spread over the top of the tart.

Bake for 25 minutes or until the topping and crust are golden brown. Remove the tart from the oven and cool for 5 minutes before serving.

Tomato Bacon Strata

Makes 6 servings

6 bacon slices
1/2 cup chopped onion
12 thin bread slices, crust removed
3 tomatoes, thinly sliced
1 tsp. salt
1/2 tsp. black pepper
1/4 tsp. dried basil
6 Swiss cheese slices, 1 oz. each
4 eggs
1 1/2 cups whole milk
1/3 cup shredded Parmesan cheese

Do not use a glass baking dish for this recipe. The difference in temperatures may cause the glass to break.

In a large skillet over medium heat, add the bacon. Cook the bacon about 7 minutes or until the bacon is crispy. Remove the bacon from the skillet and drain the bacon on paper towels. Remove all except 1 tablespoon bacon drippings from the skillet.

Add the onion to the skillet. Saute the onion for 5 minutes. Remove the skillet from the heat. Spray a 11 x 7 baking dish with non stick cooking spray. Place 6 bread slices in the bottom of the dish. Place the tomato slices over the bread. Sprinkle 1/2 teaspoon salt, black pepper and basil over the tomatoes. Spoon the onion over the tomatoes.

Crumble the bacon and sprinkle over the tomatoes. Place the Swiss cheese slices over the tomatoes. Place the remaining 6 bread slices over the cheese. In a mixing bowl, add the eggs, milk and 1/2 teaspoon salt. Whisk until well combined and pour over the bread slices. Cover the dish and chill for 4 hours.

Preheat the oven to 350°. Remove the dish from the refrigerator. Bake for 45 minutes or until the strata is set in the center. Sprinkle the Parmesan cheese over the top and bake for 5 minutes. Remove the dish from the oven and cool for 5 minutes before serving.

Steak with Tomato Onion Relish

Makes 6 servings

1 1/2 lbs. flank steak
3/4 tsp. salt
3/4 tsp. black pepper
3 tbs. olive oil
2 garlic cloves, peeled and thinly sliced
1/2 cup chicken broth
2 cups diced tomatoes
1 tsp. dried Italian seasoning
1/2 cup sliced black olives
1 tbs. balsamic vinegar
3 tbs. minced fresh parsley

Sprinkle the salt and black pepper over the flank steak. In a skillet over medium high heat, add the olive oil. When the olive oil is hot, add the flank steak. Cook for 6 minutes on each side or until the steak is done to your taste. Remove the steak from the skillet and set aside to rest.

Add the garlic to the skillet. Saute the garlic for 1 minute. Add the chicken broth, tomatoes, Italian seasoning, olives and balsamic vinegar to the skillet. Stir until all the ingredients are combined. Simmer for 6 minutes or until the liquid is reduced by half. Remove the skillet from the heat.

Thinly slice the flank steak and place the steak on a platter. Spoon the tomato relish over the top of the steak. Sprinkle the parsley over the top and serve.

Tomato Shrimp Creole Skillet

Makes 6 servings

1/2 cup green bell pepper
1/2 cup chopped onion
1/2 cup chopped celery
1 tbs. olive oil
1 garlic clove, minced
4 cups diced tomatoes
2 tsp. Tabasco sauce
1 tsp. Creole seasoning
1 lb. fresh shrimp, peeled and deveined
3 cups hot cooked rice

In a large skillet over medium heat, add the green bell pepper, onion, celery and olive oil. Saute the vegetables for 6 minutes or until they are tender. Add the garlic and saute the garlic for 1 minute. Add the tomatoes, Tabasco sauce and Creole seasoning. Stir until all the ingredients are combined.

Place a lid on the skillet and bring the tomatoes to a boil. When the vegetables are boiling, reduce the heat to low. Stir occasionally and cook for 15 minutes. Add the shrimp to the skillet. Cook for 5 minutes or until the shrimp turn pink. Remove the skillet from the heat.

Place the rice on a serving platter. Spoon the shrimp and vegetables over the rice and serve. Serve with additional Creole seasoning or Tabasco sauce if desired.

Mediterranean Chicken

Makes 4 servings

1 lb. boneless skinless chicken breast, cubed
8 garlic cloves, minced
4 tbs. olive oil
4 cups diced tomatoes
1/2 cup kalamata olives, chopped
1 tsp. dried parsley flakes
1 tsp. dried basil
1 tsp. dried oregano
2/3 cup crumbled feta cheese
8 oz. dry penne pasta, hot and cooked

In a Ziploc bag, add the chicken, garlic and olive oil. Close the bag and shake until all the ingredients are combined. Refrigerate the chicken for 4 hours. Remove the chicken from the refrigerator.

In a large skillet over medium heat, add the chicken with any marinade. Stir constantly and cook for 5 minutes or until the chicken is no longer pink. Remove the chicken from the skillet and set aside.

Add the tomatoes, olives, parsley, basil and oregano to the skillet. Stir constantly and cook for 4 minutes. Add the chicken, feta cheese and pasta to the skillet. Toss until all the ingredients are combined. Remove the skillet from the heat and serve.

Stuffed Fried Green Tomato Casserole

Makes 6 servings

2 eggs
3/4 cup whole milk
1 cup freshly grated Parmesan cheese
2 cups dry breadcrumbs
6 green tomatoes, cut into 1/4" thick slices
1 1/2 cups Bisquick
1 1/4 cups olive oil
14 oz. can crushed tomatoes
1 cup tomato sauce
6 oz. tomato paste
1/2 cup dry red wine
2 tbs. granulated sugar
1 tsp. dried basil
1 tsp. dried oregano
3/4 tsp. salt
1/2 tsp. black pepper
2 garlic cloves, minced
Additional salt and black pepper to taste
2 1/2 cups shredded mozzarella cheese

In a shallow bowl, add the eggs and milk. Whisk until well combined. In a shallow dish, add the Parmesan cheese and breadcrumbs. Stir until well combined. Place the Bisquick in a shallow dish. Dredge each tomato slice in the Bisquick. Dip each slice in the egg wash allowing the excess liquid to drip off back in the bowl. Dredge each tomato slice in the breadcrumbs. Save any remaining breadcrumbs.

In a large skillet over medium heat, add the olive oil. You will need to fry the tomatoes in batches. When the oil is hot, add the tomato slices. Fry for 2 minutes on each side or until the tomatoes are golden brown. Remove the tomatoes from the oil and drain on paper towels. Sprinkle salt and black pepper to taste over the tomatoes.

Stuffed Fried Green Tomato Casserole cont'd

While the tomatoes are cooking, make the sauce. In a sauce pan over medium heat, add the crushed tomatoes, tomato sauce, tomato paste, red wine, granulated sugar, basil, oregano, 3/4 teaspoon salt, 1/2 teaspoon black pepper and garlic. Stir until all the ingredients are combined. Bring the sauce to a boil and reduce the heat to low. Stir occasionally and simmer the sauce for 15 minutes. Remove the sauce from the heat.

Preheat the oven to 350°. Spray a 9 x 13 baking dish with non stick cooking spray. Place half the green tomatoes in the baking dish. Spoon 1 1/2 cups sauce over the tomatoes. Sprinkle 1 1/4 cups mozzarella cheese over the tomatoes. Place another layer of tomatoes over the sauce. Sprinkle 1 1/4 cups mozzarella cheese over the top. Spoon the remaining sauce around the tomatoes. Do not pour the sauce over the tomatoes. Sprinkle any remaining breadcrumbs over the top of the dish.

Bake for 40 minutes. Remove the dish from the oven. Cool for 10 minutes before serving.

Tomato Topped Halibut

Makes 6 servings

1 1/2 cups water
2 tbs. fresh lemon juice
6 halibut fillets, 6 oz. each
Black pepper to taste
1/2 cup finely chopped onion
2 large tomatoes, sliced
1/2 cup chopped green bell pepper
1/2 cup seasoned breadcrumbs
1/4 cup freshly grated Parmesan cheese
1/2 tsp. dried basil
1 tbs. vegetable oil

In a mixing bowl, add the water and lemon juice. Stir until combined and add the fish fillets to the bowl. Soak the fish for 5 minutes. Drain all the water from the fish and pat the fish dry with paper towels.

Preheat the oven to 375°. Spray a 11 x 7 baking dish with non stick cooking spray. Place the fish fillets in the baking dish. Season the fillets with black pepper to taste.

In a mixing bowl, add the onion, tomatoes, green bell pepper, breadcrumbs, Parmesan cheese, basil and vegetable oil. Toss until all the ingredients are combined. Spoon the mixture over the top of the fish fillets. Bake for 20 minutes or until the fish flakes easily with a fork. Remove the fillets from the oven and serve.

Grilled Meatless Margherita Pizzas

Makes 4 servings

1 tbs. olive oil
1 garlic clove, minced
1/2 tsp. season salt
4 flour tortillas, 8" size
1 1/2 cups finely shredded mozzarella cheese
4 cups thinly sliced tomatoes
1/4 cup sliced fresh basil leaves

In a small bowl, add the olive oil and garlic. Stir until combined and brush on one side of the flour tortillas. Sprinkle the season salt over the non oil side of the tortillas. Place one cup tomatoes on each tortilla over the season salt. Sprinkle the mozzarella cheese over the tomatoes.

Have your grill hot and ready. Place the tortillas, oil side down, on the grill. Close the grill and cook for 4 minutes or until the cheese melts and the tortillas begin to brown. Remove the tortillas from the grill and sprinkle the basil over the top before serving.

Grilled Tomato Pizza

Makes 6 servings

1 can refrigerated pizza crust
1 tbs. olive oil
1 garlic clove, peeled and halved
1 1/4 cups chopped and seeded tomato
1/2 cup shredded mozzarella cheese
3/4 cup crumbled goat cheese

Spray a large cookie sheet with non stick cooking spray. Unroll the pizza crust and place on the cookie sheet. Brush the olive oil over the top of the pizza crust. Have your grill hot and ready. Carefully slide the pizza crust off the cookie sheet and place the pizza crust on the grill. Cook for 2 minutes or until the pizza crust is golden brown. Carefully flip the pizza crust over and cook for 2 minutes.

The pizza crust will not be done at this point. Remove the crust from the grill and place back on the cookie sheet. Rub the garlic all over the top of the pizza crust. Discard the garlic cloves when finished. Sprinkle the tomato, mozzarella cheese and goat cheese over the pizza crust.

Carefully slide the crust from the pan back on the grill. Close the lid and cook for 4 minutes or until the pizza crust is done and the cheeses melted. Remove the pizza from the grill and serve.

Fresh Tomato Fettuccine

Makes 4 servings

1/2 lb. bacon, diced
2 1/2 cups chopped onion
5 cups fresh tomatoes, peeled and chopped
3 garlic cloves, minced
2 tsp. dried tarragon
1/2 tsp. salt
1/4 tsp. black pepper
1/8 tsp. cayenne pepper
1/4 cup minced fresh parsley
1 lb. fresh fettuccine, hot and cooked
1/2 cup freshly shredded Parmesan cheese

In a skillet over medium heat, add the bacon. Cook the bacon for 6 minutes or until the bacon is crisp. Remove the bacon from the skillet and drain on paper towels. Leave the bacon drippings in the skillet.

Add the onion to the skillet. Saute the onion for 10 minutes or until the onion is tender. Add the tomatoes and garlic to the skillet. Saute the tomatoes and garlic for 5 minutes. Add the tarragon, salt, black pepper and cayenne pepper to the skillet. Stir until combined. Reduce the heat to low and simmer the sauce for 20 minutes. Add the parsley and simmer the sauce for 5 minutes. Remove the pan from the heat and stir in the bacon.

Place the fettuccine on a serving platter. Spoon the sauce over the fettuccine. Sprinkle the Parmesan cheese over the top and serve.

Tomato Eggplant Bake

Makes 6 servings

1 eggplant, peeled and cut into 1/2" slices
1 large tomato, sliced
1 onion, thinly sliced
6 tbs. melted unsalted butter
1/2 tsp. dried basil
1/2 cup dry breadcrumbs
4 mozzarella cheese slices, cut into thirds
2 tbs. grated Parmesan cheese
Salt to taste

Place the eggplant slices in a colander. Sprinkle salt to taste over the eggplant. Place the colander over a bowl and let the eggplant drain for 30 minutes. Rinse the eggplant and pat the slices dry with a paper towel if needed.

Preheat the oven to 450°. Spray a 9 x 13 casserole dish with non stick cooking spray. Place the eggplant slices, in a single layer, in the bottom of the casserole dish. Place the tomato slices over the eggplant. Place the onion slices over the tomato. Sprinkle salt to taste over the vegetables. Drizzle 4 tablespoons melted butter over the vegetables.

Sprinkle the basil over the vegetables. In a small bowl, add the breadcrumbs and 2 tablespoons butter. Toss until the breadcrumbs are coated in the butter. Sprinkle the breadcrumbs over the vegetables. Lay the mozzarella cheese slices over the top of the dish. Sprinkle the Parmesan cheese over the mozzarella cheese.

Bake for 30 minutes. Remove the dish from the oven and cool for 5 minutes before serving.

Tomato Onion Salmon

Makes 4 servings

4 salmon fillets, 5 oz. each
3 tsp. olive oil
1/4 tsp. dried dill
1/4 tsp. black pepper
2 tomatoes, thinly sliced
1 onion, thinly sliced
4 garlic cloves, minced
1/2 cup chicken broth
1 tbs. fresh lemon juice
2 tbs. minced fresh parsley

Preheat the oven to 350°. Spray a 9 x 13 baking dish with non stick cooking spray. Place the fillets, skin side down, in the baking dish. Brush 2 teaspoons olive oil over the fillets. Sprinkle the dill and black pepper over the fillets. Place the tomato slices over the fillets.

In a small skillet over medium heat, add 1 teaspoon olive oil. When the oil is hot, add the onion and garlic. Saute the onion for 2 minutes. Add the chicken broth, lemon juice and parsley to the skillet. Stir until combined and cook for 3 minutes or until most of the liquid has evaporated. Remove the skillet from the heat.

Spoon the onion and garlic over the salmon fillets. Bake for 15 minutes or until the fillets flake easily with a fork. Remove the fillets from the oven and serve.

Sausage Tomato Pasta Skillet

Makes 4 servings

1 lb. ground Italian sausage
5 cups diced tomatoes
1/2 tsp. dried basil
12 oz. pkg. dry pasta, hot and cooked
Salt and black pepper to taste
Parmesan cheese to taste

Use your favorite shape pasta for this recipe. In a large skillet over medium heat, add the Italian sausage. Stir frequently to break the sausage into crumbles as it cooks. Cook for 7 minutes or until the sausage is well browned and no longer pink. Drain any excess grease from the skillet.

Add the tomatoes and basil to the skillet. Season to taste with salt and black pepper. Stir until all the ingredients are combined. Cook for 10-12 minutes or until the tomatoes are tender. Remove the skillet from the heat and stir in the hot cooked pasta. Sprinkle Parmesan cheese to taste over the top of the pasta and serve.

Tomato & Parmesan Gnocchi

Makes 4 servings

1 garlic bulb
2 tbs. olive oil
10 fresh sage leaves
16 oz. pkg. gnocchi
4 cups chicken broth
1 1/2 cups chopped fresh tomatoes
1/2 tsp. black pepper
2 tbs. freshly grated Parmesan cheese

Cut off the pointed end of the garlic bulb. Place the garlic on a sheet of aluminum foil. Place the foil on a baking sheet. Preheat the oven to 350°. Bake for 1 hour. Remove the garlic from the oven. Squeeze the garlic from the bulb into a mixing bowl. Using a fork, mash the garlic cloves.

In a small skillet over medium heat, add the olive oil and sage leaves. Cook for 2 minutes or until the sage leaves are crisp. Remove the skillet from the heat. Remove the sage leaves from the skillet but leave the oil in the skillet. Drain the sage leaves on paper towels.

Cook the gnocchi according to package directions using the chicken broth instead of water for the cooking liquid. Drain the gnocchi but save 1/4 cup cooking liquid for use later in the recipe.

Add the gnocchi, oil from the skillet, 1/4 cup cooking liquid, tomatoes and black pepper to the bowl with the garlic. Toss until all the ingredients are combined. Spoon the gnocchi onto a serving platter. Sprinkle the Parmesan cheese and sage leaves over the top before serving.

Fresh Tomato Prosciutto Penne

Makes 6 servings

1/4 lb. prosciutto, chopped
1/4 cup olive oil
3 cups diced tomatoes
4 garlic cloves, minced
1/4 cup toasted pine nuts
1/4 cup chopped fresh oregano
1/2 tsp. dried crushed red pepper flakes
1/4 tsp. granulated sugar
1/4 tsp. black pepper
1/8 tsp. salt
16 oz. pkg. dry penne pasta, hot and cooked
Parmesan cheese to taste

In a skillet over medium heat, add the prosciutto and olive oil. Saute the prosciutto for 7 minutes or until the prosciutto is crisp. Add the tomatoes, garlic, pine nuts, oregano, red pepper flakes, granulated sugar, black pepper and salt to the skillet. Stir until well combined and cook for 5 minutes. Remove the skillet from the heat.

Place the penne pasta on a serving platter. Spoon the tomatoes and prosciutto over the pasta. Sprinkle Parmesan cheese to taste over the top and serve.

Fresh Tomato Mushroom Pasta

Makes 6 servings

16 oz. pkg. dry pasta, hot and cooked
1/2 cup chopped onion
2 garlic cloves, minced
2 tbs. olive oil
2 cups chopped and seeded tomatoes
4 cups sliced fresh mushrooms
3/4 tsp. salt
1/4 tsp. crushed red pepper flakes
1/2 cup whipping cream
3 oz. cream cheese, cubed
3 tbs. chopped fresh basil
3 tbs. grated Romano cheese

In a large skillet over medium heat, add the onion, garlic and olive oil. Saute the onion and garlic for 5 minutes or until they are tender. Add the tomatoes, mushrooms, salt and red pepper flakes to the skillet. Saute the mushrooms for 10 minutes.

Add the whipping cream, cream cheese and basil to the skillet. Stir constantly and cook until the cream cheese melts. Remove the skillet from the heat. Place the pasta on a serving platter. Spoon the sauce over the pasta. Sprinkle the Romano cheese over the top and serve.

Greek Tomato Sauce with Penne

Makes 6 servings

6 cups chopped fresh tomatoes
12 oz. jar marinated artichokes, drained and chopped
1/2 cup sliced black olives
1/3 cup sliced green onion
4 oz. feta cheese, crumbled
1/3 cup olive oil
2 tbs. red wine vinegar
2 tbs. chopped fresh parsley
1 tbs. chopped fresh basil
1 tsp. granulated sugar
2 tsp. Greek seasoning
1/4 tsp. salt
1/4 tsp. black pepper
12 oz. dry penne pasta, hot and cooked

In a mixing bowl, add the tomatoes, artichokes, black olives, green onion and half the feta cheese. Toss until all the ingredients are combined. In a jar with a lid, add the olive oil, red wine vinegar, parsley, basil, granulated sugar, Greek seasoning, salt and black pepper. Place the lid on the jar and shake until all the ingredients are blended.

Pour the dressing over the tomatoes. Toss until the tomatoes are coated in the dressing. Cover the bowl and refrigerate for 2 hours. Place the hot penne pasta on a serving platter. Spoon the tomatoes and dressing over the pasta. Sprinkle the remaining feta cheese over the top and serve.

Red Wine Tomato Pasta

Makes 6 servings

1 1/2 tsp. minced garlic
2 tbs. olive oil
1/2 cup dry red wine
4 cups diced tomatoes with any juice
1 tsp. dried basil
1/2 tsp. dried oregano
1 tsp. granulated sugar
1/4 tsp. black pepper
12 oz. pkg. thin spaghetti noodles, hot and cooked
1 cup shredded mozzarella cheese
1/3 cup freshly grated Parmesan cheese
1/4 cup minced fresh basil

In a skillet over medium heat, add the garlic and olive oil. Saute the garlic for 1 minute. Add the red wine, tomatoes, basil, oregano, granulated sugar and black pepper. Stir until all the ingredients are combined. Bring the sauce to a boil. When the sauce is boiling, reduce the heat to low. Stir occasionally and simmer the sauce for 20 minutes. The sauce will thicken as it cooks. Remove the skillet from the heat.

In a serving bowl, add the spaghetti noodles, mozzarella cheese and Parmesan cheese. Toss until the noodles are coated in the cheese. Pour the sauce over the noodles. Sprinkle the basil over the top and serve.

Spicy Tomato Vermicelli

Makes 4 servings

6 garlic cloves, minced
2 tbs. olive oil
4 jalapeno peppers, seeded and minced
4 1/2 cups chopped tomato
1/2 tsp. salt
1/2 cup chopped fresh basil
8 oz. pkg. dry vermicelli, hot and cooked
Parmesan cheese to taste

In a large skillet over medium heat, add the garlic and olive oil. Saute the garlic for 2 minutes. Add the jalapeno peppers to the skillet. Saute the peppers for 1 minute. Add the tomatoes and salt to the skillet. Saute the tomatoes for 4 minutes. Add the basil to the skillet and toss until all the ingredients are combined. Remove the skillet from the heat.

Place the vermicelli on a serving platter. Spoon the tomatoes and garlic over the pasta. Sprinkle the to taste with Parmesan cheese and serve.

Fresh Tomato Linguine

Makes 4 servings

6 tbs. chopped fresh parsley
4 tsp. grated lemon zest
1 1/2 tsp. minced garlic
1 tbs. olive oil
6 cups diced tomatoes
1/2 tsp. black pepper
1/4 tsp. salt
1 tbs. fresh lemon juice
12 oz. pkg. dry linguine, hot and cooked
Additional olive oil for drizzling, optional

In a small bowl, add 4 tablespoons parsley, 3 teaspoons lemon zest and 1/2 teaspoon garlic. Stir until combined and set aside for use later in the recipe. In a large skillet over medium heat, add 1 teaspoon garlic and the olive oil. Saute the garlic for 1 minute.

Add 4 cups tomatoes, salt and black pepper to the skillet. Saute the tomatoes for 10 minutes. Add 2 tablespoons parsley, 1 teaspoon lemon zest and lemon juice to the skillet. Stir constantly and cook for 1 minute. Stir in 2 cups tomatoes.

Place the linguine on a serving platter. Spoon the sauce over the linguine. Drizzle with additional olive oil if desired.

Grilled Tomato Feta Chicken

Makes 4 servings

4 boneless skinless chicken breast, 6 oz. each
1 tbs. vegetable oil
1/2 tsp. garlic pepper seasoning
8 slices fresh tomato, 1/2" thick
1/2 cup tomato basil feta cheese
1/4 cup chopped fresh basil

Have your grill hot and ready. Brush the vegetable oil over the chicken breast. Sprinkle the garlic pepper over the chicken. Place the chicken on the grill and cook for 2 minutes. Turn the chicken breast over.

Place 2 tomato slices on each chicken breast. Close the lid and cook for 5 minutes or until the chicken is no longer pink and tender. Remove the chicken from the grill and place on a serving platter. Sprinkle the tomato basil feta cheese and basil over the chicken. Let the chicken rest for 5 minutes before serving.

Green Tomato Gumbo

Makes 16 servings

3/4 cup vegetable oil
3/4 cup all purpose flour
1 green bell pepper, finely chopped
2 cups finely chopped onion
2 celery ribs, finely chopped
4 jalapeno peppers, finely chopped
6 garlic cloves, minced
1 tbs. green Tabasco sauce
4 tbs. fresh lime juice
1 tbs. Cajun seasoning
5 1/4 cups chicken broth
8 cups green tomatoes, cored and chopped
1 lb. Cajun smoked sausage, cut into 1/4" slices
2 bay leaves
Salt and black pepper to taste
16 oz. pkg. frozen cut okra
1 lb. fresh shrimp, peeled and deveined
1 cup fresh cilantro, chopped
1 tbs. file' powder
8 bacon slices, cooked and crumbled
2 2/3 cups dry long grain rice, cooked

In a large dutch oven over high heat, add the vegetable oil. When the oil is hot, stir in the all purpose flour. Stir constantly and cook for 5 minutes or until the roux is copper colored. Reduce the heat to medium.

Add the green bell pepper, onion, celery, jalapeno peppers, garlic, Tabasco sauce, lime juice and Cajun seasoning. Stir constantly and cook for 3 minutes. Add the chicken broth, green tomatoes, smoked sausage and bay leaves. Stir constantly and bring the gumbo to a boil. Reduce the heat to low and simmer for 45 minutes. Stir occasionally while the gumbo is simmering. Remove the bay leaves from the gumbo. Skim off any fat that rises to the top.

Green Tomato Gumbo cont'd

Season the gumbo to taste with salt and black pepper. Add the okra to the pan. Simmer the okra for 15 minutes. Stir in the shrimp, cilantro and file' powder. Stir until combined and cook for 4 minutes or until the shrimp turn pink. Remove the pan from the heat.

Spoon the rice into serving bowls. Spoon the gumbo over the top of the rice. Sprinkle the bacon over the top and serve.

Great Northern Beans with Tomatoes

Makes 6 servings

1 lb. dry great northern beans
7 cups water
1/4 lb. salt pork
1 tsp. salt
4 cups diced fresh tomatoes
4 green onions, sliced
1 tbs. molasses
Hot cornbread

In a dutch oven over medium heat, add the great northern beans, water and salt pork. Bring the beans to a boil and place a lid on the pan. Reduce the heat to low and simmer the beans for 3 hours or until the beans are tender. Add water as needed to keep the beans covered in water.

Remove the salt pork from the beans and discard. Add the tomatoes, green onions and molasses. Stir until combined and cook for 10 minutes. Remove the pan from the heat and serve the beans with hot cornbread.

3 BREADS & SANDWICHES

Tomatoes add a wonderful touch to homemade breads. Tomatoes are always great on sandwiches but try sandwiches where tomatoes are the star ingredient.

Savory Tomato Biscuit Bites

Makes 12 servings

2 cups Bisquick
1/3 cup grated Parmesan cheese
1 tbs. granulated sugar
1 tsp. dried Italian seasoning
1/4 tsp. cayenne pepper
2/3 cup mayonnaise
1/4 cup whole milk
3 fresh tomatoes, thinly sliced
10 bacon slices, cooked and crumbled
1/4 cup thinly sliced green onion
Salt and black pepper to taste

Preheat the oven to 425°. In a mixing bowl, add the Bisquick, Parmesan cheese, granulated sugar, Italian seasoning, cayenne pepper, 1/3 cup mayonnaise and milk. Whisk until combined and a soft dough forms.

Spray a baking sheet with non stick cooking spray. Press the dough onto the baking sheet to form a crust. Bake for 8 minutes or until the biscuits are done and golden brown. Remove the biscuits from the oven.

Immediately spread 1/3 cup mayonnaise over the hot biscuits. Place the tomato slices over the mayonnaise. Sprinkle the bacon and green onion over the tomatoes. Season to taste with salt and black pepper. Cut into pieces and serve.

Tomato Basil Drop Biscuits

Makes 18 biscuits

1 tbs. unsalted butter
1/2 cup finely chopped green onion
1 tbs. vegetable oil
3/4 cup chopped tomato, seeded
1/4 cup minced fresh basil
2 cups all purpose flour
1 tbs. baking powder
1 tsp. salt
1/4 tsp. black pepper
1/3 cup vegetable shortening
2/3 cup whole milk

Preheat the oven to 425°. Grease a large baking sheet with the butter. In a skillet over medium heat, add the green onion and vegetable oil. Saute the green onion for 3 minutes. Add the tomato and saute the tomato for 1 minute. Remove the skillet from the heat and stir in the basil. Cool the vegetables for 5 minutes.

In a mixing bowl, add the all purpose flour, baking powder, salt and black pepper. Stir until well combined. Add the vegetable shortening to the dry ingredients. Using a pastry blender, cut the shortening into the dry ingredients until you have coarse crumbs. Add the milk and vegetables from the skillet to the bowl. Stir only until the batter is moistened and combined.

Drop the biscuits by tablespoonfuls on your baking sheet. Space the biscuits about 2" apart. Bake for 10 minutes or until the biscuits are golden brown. Remove the biscuits from the oven and serve.

Fresh Tomato Biscuits

Makes 8 biscuits

1/4 cup mayonnaise
1/4 tsp. salt
1/4 tsp. black pepper
1/4 cup shredded fresh basil
8 ct. can refrigerated biscuits (Grand's)
2 fresh tomatoes, thinly sliced

In a small bowl, add the mayonnaise, salt, black pepper and basil. Stir until well combined. Preheat the oven to 400°. Press each biscuit into a 4" circle. Spray a baking sheet with non stick cooking spray. Place each biscuit on the baking sheet.

Bake the biscuits for 6 minutes. Spread the mayonnaise over the top of the biscuits. Place the tomato slices over the mayonnaise. Bake for 6 minutes or until the biscuits are done and golden brown. Remove the biscuits from the oven and serve.

Tomato Parmesan Journey Cakes

Makes 20 cakes

2 cups cold cooked basmati rice
2 eggs, beaten
2 cups whole milk
2 cups all purpose flour
1 1/2 tbs. unsalted butter, melted
2 tsp. salt
1 cup finely chopped tomato
1/2 cup shredded Parmesan cheese
1/4 cup minced kalamata olives
Peanut oil for frying

In a mixing bowl, add the rice, eggs, milk, all purpose flour, butter, salt, tomato, Parmesan cheese and olives. Stir only until the batter is moistened and combined.

You will need to cook the journey cakes in batches. Add oil as needed to maintain the temperature and depth of the oil. The temperature of the oil should be about 350° when ready.

In a skillet over medium heat, add peanut oil to a depth of 1/4" in the skillet. When the oil is hot, use 1/4 cup batter for each cake. Drop the batter into the hot oil. Cook for 2 minutes on each side or until the cakes are golden brown. Remove the cakes from the skillet and drain on paper towels.

Tomato Rosemary Focaccia

Makes 6 servings

10 oz. can refrigerated pizza crust
2 tbs. olive oil
2 garlic cloves, minced
1/4 tsp. salt
1 tbs. minced fresh rosemary
2 tomatoes, seeded and thinly sliced
1/2 cup thinly sliced purple onion

Spray a 9 x 13 baking sheet with non stick cooking spray. Unroll the pizza crust from the can and spread the crust on the baking sheet. In a small bowl, add the olive oil, garlic, salt and half the rosemary. Stir until combined and brush over the pizza crust.

Place the tomatoes and onion over the pizza crust. Sprinkle the remaining rosemary over the top. Preheat the oven to 425°. Bake for 15 minutes or until the crust is golden brown. Remove the bread from the oven and serve.

BLT Muffins

Makes 12 muffins

2 cups all purpose flour
1 tbs. baking powder
1 tbs. granulated sugar
1 cup whole milk
1/2 cup full fat mayonnaise
3/4 cup cooked and crumbled bacon
1/2 cup seeded and diced tomato
2 tbs. minced fresh parsley
1 cup seeded and diced tomatoes, optional
Softened cream cheese, optional

Preheat the oven to 400°. Spray a 12 count muffin tin with non stick cooking spray. In a mixing bowl, add the all purpose flour, baking powder and granulated sugar. Stir until combined. Add the milk and mayonnaise to the dry ingredients. Stir only until the batter is moistened.

Gently stir in the bacon, 1/2 cup tomatoes and parsley. Stir only until combined. Do not over mix the batter or the muffins will be tough. Spoon the batter into the muffin cups filling them about 2/3 full.

Bake for 20 minutes or until a toothpick inserted in the center of the muffins comes out clean. Remove the muffins from the oven. Cool the muffins in the pan for 5 minutes. Remove the muffins from the pan. Split the muffins and spread with cream cheese if desired. Sprinkle 1 cup diced tomatoes over the cream cheese if desired.

Cilantro Lime Tomato Griddle Cake Sandwiches

Makes 8 sandwiches

4 bacon slices
1 cup finely chopped fresh okra
1 1/2 cups self rising white cornmeal
1/2 cup all purpose flour
1 tbs. granulated sugar
1 2/3 cups buttermilk
3 tbs. melted unsalted butter
2 beaten eggs
1 cup mayonnaise
1 cup fresh cilantro leaves
1 tsp. grated lime zest
1 tbs. fresh lime juice
1 garlic clove, minced
16 tomato slices, 1/2" thick

In a skillet over medium heat, add the bacon. Cook for 8 minutes or until the bacon is crispy. Remove the bacon from the skillet and drain on paper towels. Leave the bacon drippings in the skillet. Finely chop the bacon.

Add the okra to the skillet. Saute the okra for 3 minutes or until the okra is crisp tender. Remove the skillet from the heat. In a mixing bowl, add the cornmeal, all purpose flour and granulated sugar. Whisk until the dry ingredients are combined. Add the bacon, okra with any pan drippings, buttermilk, butter and eggs to the bowl. Whisk until the batter is well combined.

Spray a large griddle with non stick cooking spray. Set the griddle temperature to 350°. Spoon 1/4 cup batter for each griddle cake on the griddle. Cook for 3 minutes or until the top is covered in bubbles and the bottom golden brown. Flip the cake over and cook for 2 minutes or until the griddle cakes are done. Remove the griddle cakes and keep warm while you prepare the dressing. You need 16 griddle cakes for this recipe.

Cilantro Lime Tomato Griddle Sandwiches cont'd

In a blender, add the mayonnaise, cilantro, lime zest, lime juice and garlic. Process until smooth and combined. Spread the mayonnaise on one side of each griddle cake. Place two tomato slices on 8 griddle cakes. Place the remaining griddle cakes on top and serve.

Grilled Open Faced Summer Sandwiches

Makes 4 servings

2 large tomatoes, cut into 1/2" slices
1 tsp. salt
1/2 tsp. black pepper
4 French bread slices, about 1" thick
1/4 cup olive oil
2 onions, cut into 1/2" slices
1/2 cup mayonnaise
3 tbs. prepared pesto
1 cup sliced black olives

Place the tomatoes slices on paper towels. Sprinkle the salt and black pepper over the tomatoes. Let the tomatoes drain on the paper towels while you prepare the sandwiches.

Brush the olive oil over both sides of the bread slices. Place the French bread slices on a hot grill. Grill for 2 minutes on each side or until the bread is toasted. Add the onion slices to the grill and cook about 4 minutes on each side or until the onion slices are tender. Remove the bread and onions from the grill.

In a small bowl, add the mayonnaise and pesto. Stir until combined and spread on one side of each bread slice. Place the bread slices, mayonnaise pesto side up, on a serving plate. Place the tomato and onion slices over the bread. Sprinkle the black olives over the top and serve.

Fried Green Tomato Sandwiches

Makes 8 servings

1 cup fine dry breadcrumbs
2 tbs. grated Parmesan cheese
1/2 tsp. salt
Pinch of cayenne pepper
4 large green tomatoes, cut into 1/4" slices
2 eggs, beaten
1/4 cup unsalted butter
8 lettuce leaves
1 onion, thinly sliced
16 oz. pkg. bacon, cooked until crisp
8 sandwich rolls, split
1/3 cup ranch dressing

In a small bowl, add the breadcrumbs, Parmesan cheese, salt and cayenne pepper. Stir until well combined. Place the beaten eggs in a small bowl. Dip each tomato slice in the egg allowing the excess egg to drip off back into the bowl. Dredge each tomato slice in the breadcrumbs.

In a skillet over medium heat, add the butter. When the butter melts, add the tomato slices to the skillet. You will have to fry the tomatoes in batches. Cook the tomatoes about 3 minutes on each side or until they are golden brown. Remove the tomatoes from the skillet and drain on paper towels.

Spread the ranch dressing on one side of each roll. Place a lettuce leaf over the dressing. Place the onion slices and bacon slices over the lettuce. Place the green tomatoes over the bacon. Place the top roll over the filling and serve.

Bacon Tomato Melts

Makes 4 servings

4 onion bagels, split and toasted
8 tomato slices, 1/2" thick
8 bacon slices, cooked
1 cup shredded mozzarella cheese
1 cup prepared ranch dressing

Preheat the oven to the broiler position. Place the bagels, cut side up, on a baking sheet. Place one tomato slice on each bagel. Cut each bacon slice into two pieces. Place two pieces bacon over the tomatoes. Sprinkle the mozzarella cheese over the bacon.

Broil for 2 minutes or until the cheese is bubbly and melted. Remove the sandwiches from the oven. Spread ranch dressing over the top and serve.

Eggplant, Tomato & Feta Flatbreads

Makes 4 servings

1 small eggplant, cut into six 1/2" slices
Salt to taste
2 garlic cloves, minced
2 tbs. olive oil
3 fresh tomatoes, sliced
1 cup fresh basil leaves
4 flatbread rounds
3 oz. crumbled feta cheese
1 1/2 tbs. white balsamic vinegar
1/2 tsp. black pepper

Place the eggplant slices on paper towels. Sprinkle salt to taste over the slices. Let the eggplant slices rest for 1 hour at room temperature. In a small bowl, add the garlic and olive oil. Stir until combined and let the garlic sit at room temperature for 5 minutes.

Rinse the eggplant with water and pat the slices dry. Brush the garlic olive oil over the eggplant slices and tomato slices. Place the eggplant slices on a baking sheet. Turn the oven to the broiler position. Broil the eggplant for 3 minutes on each side. Remove the eggplant from the oven and cool.

Place the basil leaves over the top of the flatbread rounds. Sprinkle the feta cheese over the flatbreads. Place the eggplant and tomato slices over the top of the flatbreads. Drizzle each flatbread with white balsamic vinegar. Sprinkle the black pepper over the top and serve.

Grilled Gruyere Tomato Sandwiches

Makes 6 servings

12 slices French bread, about 3/4" thick
3 tbs. olive oil
1/2 cup sliced black olives
2 large fresh tomatoes, seeded and thinly sliced
6 oz. Gruyere cheese, sliced
1/3 cup chopped fresh basil leaves

Have your grill hot and ready. Brush both sides of the bread slices with the olive oil. Place the olives, tomatoes, Gruyere cheese and basil on one side of the bread. Place the bread slices, topping side up, on the grill. Close the grill lid and cook about 5 minutes or until the cheese is melted and the bread toasted.

Remove the bread from the grill and serve.

Open Face Crab Tomato Sandwiches

Makes 6 servings

1 egg, beaten
3 oz. pkg. cream cheese, softened
1 tsp. lemon juice
2 tbs. chopped fresh parsley
2 tbs. grated Parmesan cheese
3 tbs. mayonnaise
1 cup cooked lump crab meat
6 slices bread, crust removed
2 large tomatoes

Slice each tomato into 3 slices. In a mixing bowl, add the egg, cream cheese, lemon juice, parsley, Parmesan cheese and mayonnaise. Stir until well combined. Gently stir in the crab meat.

Place the bread slices on a baking pan. Preheat the oven to 350°. Place the bread in the oven until lightly toasted. Remove the pan from the oven. Turn the oven to the broiler position. Place one tomato slice on top of each bread slice. Spread the crab mixture over the tomato slices. Broil for 2 minutes or until the sandwiches are hot and lightly browned. Remove the sandwiches from the oven and serve.

Tomato Egg Sandwiches

These sandwiches are perfect for brunch or weekends.

Makes 12 sandwiches

8 oz. pkg. cream cheese, softened
9 oz. jar horseradish sauce
1/4 cup grated onion
1 oz. pkg. dry ranch dressing mix
24 bread slices, toasted
24 tomato slices, 1/2" thick
8 hard boiled eggs, cut into slices
Salt and black pepper to season

In a mixing bowl, add the cream cheese, horseradish sauce, onion and dry ranch dressing mix. Using a mixer on medium speed, beat until the spread is smooth and creamy.

Spread the mixture on one side of each bread slice. Place two tomato slices and the egg slices over the spread on 12 bread slices. Season to taste with salt and black pepper. Place the remaining bread slices over the top and serve.

You can make the spread and hard boiled eggs up to 24 hours in advance. Refrigerate the spread and eggs until ready to serve. Do not slice the eggs until ready to serve.

4 SIDE DISHES & SALADS

Tomatoes are famously known for salads and fried green tomatoes. Included are our favorite salad and side dish recipes.

Fried Green Tomatoes

Makes 6 servings

4 green tomatoes
1 tsp. salt
1/4 tsp. lemon pepper seasoning
3/4 cup plain white or yellow cornmeal
1/2 cup vegetable oil

Slice the tomatoes into 1/4" slices. Place the tomato slices on paper towels. Sprinkle the salt and lemon pepper over the tomatoes. Let the tomatoes drain for 20 minutes.

In a shallow bowl, add the cornmeal. Dredge each tomato slice in the cornmeal. In a large skillet over medium heat, add the vegetable oil. You will need to cook the tomatoes in batches. When the oil is hot, add the tomato slices. Fry about 4 minutes on each side or until the tomatoes are golden brown. Remove the tomatoes from the skillet and drain on paper towels.

Herb Tomatoes & Green Beans

Makes 4 servings

3 green onions, chopped
2 garlic cloves, minced
2 tsp. olive oil
3 cups fresh green beans, trimmed
1/4 cup chicken broth
2 tomatoes, diced
1 tbs. minced fresh oregano
1 tbs. minced fresh parsley
1/8 tsp. salt
1/8 tsp. black pepper

In a skillet over medium heat, add the green onions, garlic and olive oil. Saute the green onions and garlic for 4 minutes. Add the green beans and chicken broth to the skillet. Bring the green beans to a boil and place a lid on the skillet. Reduce the heat to low and simmer the green beans for 10 minutes. The green beans should be crisp tender when ready.

Add the tomatoes, oregano, parsley, salt and black pepper to the skillet. Toss until all the ingredients are combined. Remove the skillet from the heat and serve.

Tomato Grits

Makes 6 servings

2 bacon slices, chopped
3 3/4 cups chicken broth
1/2 tsp. salt
1 cup quick cooking grits
2 cups diced tomatoes
4 oz. Velveeta cheese, cubed
2 tbs. minced jalapeno peppers, optional

In a sauce pan over medium heat, add the bacon. Stir frequently and cook for 5 minutes or until the bacon is crispy. Remove the bacon from the pan and drain on paper towels. Leave the bacon drippings in the pan.

Add the chicken broth and salt to the pan. Stir until combined and bring the chicken broth to a boil. When the chicken broth is boiling, stir in the grits and tomatoes. Stir constantly and bring the grits to a boil. When the grits are boiling, reduce the heat to low. Stir occasionally and cook for 15 minutes or until the grits are tender and thicken. Stir in the Velveeta cheese and jalapeno pepper. Remove the grits from the heat. Place a lid on the pan and let the grits sit for 5 minutes. The cheese should be melted. Stir until combined and serve.

Spicy Tomato Macaroni & Cheese Skillet

Makes 6 servings

8 oz. dry penne pasta, hot and cooked
1/4 cup unsalted butter
1/2 cup chopped onion
2 tbs. minced jalapeno pepper
8 oz. Mexican Velveeta cheese, cubed
1 cup sour cream
2 cups diced tomatoes

In a large skillet over medium heat, add the butter. When the butter melts, add the onion and jalapeno pepper. Saute the onion and pepper for 5 minutes. Add the Velveeta cheese to the skillet. Stir until the cheese melts.

Add the sour cream and tomatoes to the skillet. Stir until all the ingredients are combined. Add the hot cooked pasta to the skillet. Toss until the pasta is coated in the sauce. Remove the skillet from the heat and serve.

Roasted Rosemary Cherry Tomatoes

Makes 6 servings

4 cups cherry tomatoes
1 tsp. olive oil
1 1/2 tsp. chopped fresh rosemary
2 garlic cloves, minced
1/4 tsp. salt
1/4 tsp. black pepper

Preheat the oven to 425°. Spray a baking sheet with non stick cooking spray. In a Ziploc bag, add the cherry tomatoes, olive oil, rosemary, garlic, salt and black pepper. Close the bag and shake until the tomatoes are coated in the oil and seasonings.

Spread the tomatoes on the baking sheet. Bake for 15 minutes or until the tomatoes begin to burst. Remove the tomatoes from the oven and cool for 5 minutes before serving.

Basil Cherry Tomatoes

Makes 6 servings

4 cups cherry tomatoes, halved
1/2 cup chopped fresh basil
1 1/2 tsp. olive oil
Salt and black pepper to taste

Add the tomatoes, basil and olive oil to a serving bowl. Toss until all the ingredients are combined. Season to taste with salt and black pepper. Cover the bowl and chill for 1 hour before serving.

Cheesy Tomato Casserole

Makes 4 servings

6 cups chopped fresh tomatoes
1/2 cup butter cracker crumbs
1/2 cup shredded sharp cheddar cheese
1 tbs. melted unsalted butter
1/4 cup finely chopped onion
1 beaten egg
1/2 tsp. salt
1/4 tsp. paprika

Preheat the oven to 325°. Add all the ingredients to a mixing bowl. Stir until well combined. Spray an 8" square baking dish with non stick cooking spray. Spoon the casserole into the dish.

Bake for 30 minutes or until the casserole is bubbly and golden brown. Remove the dish from the oven and cool for 5 minutes before serving.

Baked Green Tomatoes

Makes 4 servings

4 green tomatoes, sliced 1/2" thick
Salt and black pepper to season
1/2 cup light brown sugar
3/4 cup butter crackers crumbs
4 tbs. unsalted butter

Preheat the oven to 350°. Spray a 2 quart shallow baking dish with non stick cooking spray. Place the tomato slices in the baking dish. Season to taste with salt and black pepper. Sprinkle the brown sugar and butter cracker crumbs over the tomatoes.

Cut the butter into small pieces. Place the butter over the tomatoes. Bake for 30 minutes or until the tomatoes are tender. Remove the tomatoes from the oven and serve.

Creole Tomatoes & Hominy

Makes 6 servings

4 cups canned hominy, drained
3 cups diced fresh tomatoes
10 oz. can diced tomatoes with green chiles
1 cup tomato sauce
15 slices bacon
1 1/2 cups chopped onion
1 cup chopped green bell pepper

In a slow cooker, add the hominy, fresh tomatoes, diced tomatoes with juice and tomato sauce. Stir until combined. In a large skillet over medium heat, add the bacon. Cook for 10 minutes or until the bacon is crispy. Remove the bacon from the skillet and drain on paper towels.

Drain all but 1 tablespoon bacon drippings from the skillet. Add the onion and green bell pepper to the skillet. Saute the vegetables for 5 minutes. Remove the skillet from the heat and spoon the onion and green bell pepper into the slow cooker. Add the bacon to the slow cooker. Stir until all the ingredients are combined.

Set the temperature to low and cook for 6 hours.

Fresh Tomato Pasta

Makes 6 servings

2 1/2 cups diced fresh tomatoes
1 tbs. dried basil
1/2 cup vegetable oil
2 tbs. cider vinegar
2 garlic cloves, minced
1/4 tsp. salt
1/8 tsp. black pepper
3 tbs. grated Parmesan cheese
8 oz. dry pasta, hot and cooked

In a mixing bowl, add the tomatoes and basil. Toss until well combined. In a small bowl, add the vegetable oil, cider vinegar, garlic, salt and black pepper. Whisk until well combined.

Place the pasta in a serving bowl. Add the tomatoes and basil to the pasta. Drizzle half the oil dressing over the pasta. Toss until all the ingredients are coated in the dressing. Use the remaining dressing to taste. Sprinkle the Parmesan cheese over the top and serve.

Tomato Spinach Saute

Makes 4 servings

16 oz. pkg. fresh spinach
1 tbs. olive oil
1/2 tsp. salt
1/2 tsp. black pepper
2 garlic cloves, minced
1 1/2 cups chopped tomato
1 tbs. balsamic vinegar
Additional salt to taste

In a large skillet over medium heat, add the olive oil. When the olive oil is hot, add the spinach. Saute the spinach for 2 minutes or until the spinach wilts. Sprinkle 1/4 teaspoon salt and black pepper over the spinach. Stir until combined. Remove the spinach from the skillet and place on a serving platter.

Add the garlic to the skillet. Saute the garlic for 1 minute. Add the tomato and saute only until the tomato is heated. Sprinkle 1/4 teaspoon salt over the tomatoes. Stir until combined and remove the skillet from the heat. Add the balsamic vinegar to the tomatoes and toss until combined. Spoon the tomatoes over the spinach. Season with additional salt to taste.

Southern Fried Okra & Green Tomatoes

Makes 8 servings

1 cup buttermilk
1 egg
1 1/2 cups plain white or yellow cornmeal
1/8 tsp. salt
1/4 tsp. black pepper
1 lb. fresh okra, sliced
3 green tomatoes, cut into bite size chunks
Vegetable oil for frying
Additional salt for seasoning

In a mixing bowl, add the buttermilk and egg. Whisk until well combined. Add the cornmeal, 1/8 teaspoon salt and black pepper. Whisk until the batter is smooth and combined.

In a deep fryer or dutch oven, add vegetable oil to a depth of 3" in the pan. The temperature of the oil should be 375°. Place the dutch oven over medium high heat. You will need to fry the okra and tomatoes in batches. Do not batter the okra and tomatoes until you are ready to fry them.

When the oil is hot, dip the okra and tomatoes in the batter allowing the excess batter to drip off back into the bowl. Drop the okra and tomatoes in the hot oil. Fry about 2 minutes per side or until the vegetables are golden brown and tender. Remove the vegetables from the hot oil and drain on paper towels. Sprinkle additional salt over the fried vegetables if desired.

Pan Fried Okra & Tomatoes

Makes 8 servings

8 cups fresh okra, halved
1/2 cup vegetable oil
1 purple onion, thinly sliced
3 tomatoes, thinly sliced
2 tbs. fresh lime juice
1 1/2 tsp. salt
1 1/2 tsp. black pepper

You will need to cook the okra in batches. Add 1/4 cup vegetable oil to a skillet over medium high heat. When the oil is hot, add 4 cups okra to the skillet. Cook for 6 minutes or until the okra is well browned. Remove the okra from the skillet and drain on paper towels. Repeat until all the okra is cooked.

In a large serving bowl, add the okra, purple onion, tomatoes, lime juice, salt and black pepper. Toss until all the ingredients are combined. Serve at room temperature.

Cheesy Baked Okra Tomato Casserole

Makes 6 servings

1/3 cup unsalted butter
1/2 cup chopped onion
1/2 cup chopped green bell pepper
1 tbs. all purpose flour
1 tsp. salt
1/2 tsp. black pepper
2 cups diced fresh tomatoes
8 oz. Velveeta cheese, cubed
1 tsp. chopped fresh basil
1 1/2 cups sliced fresh okra
3 oz. dry pasta shells, cooked
1/4 cup fine dry breadcrumbs

In a large skillet over medium high heat, add the butter, onion and green bell pepper. Saute the vegetables for 5 minutes. Add the all purpose flour, salt and black pepper to the skillet. Stir until all the ingredients are combined.

Add the tomatoes, 4 oz. Velveeta cheese and basil. Stir until the cheese melts and the tomatoes thicken. Add the okra and pasta shells to the skillet. Stir until combined and remove the skillet from the heat.

Preheat the oven to 350°. Spoon the mixture into a 1 quart casserole dish. Sprinkle the breadcrumbs over the top of the dish. Bake for 20 minutes. Place the remaining Velveeta cheese over the top. Bake for 10 minutes or until the cheese melts and is bubbly. Remove the dish from the oven and serve.

Grilled Tomatoes

Makes 4 servings

4 large tomatoes, cut into wedges
2 garlic cloves, minced
1/2 tsp. dried oregano
3 tbs. unsalted butter

Place a large piece of heavy duty aluminum foil on your work surface. Place the tomato wedges in the center of the aluminum foil. In a small skillet over medium heat, add the garlic, oregano and butter. Saute the garlic for 2 minutes. Remove the skillet from the heat and pour the butter over the tomatoes.

Wrap the aluminum foil around the tomatoes to form a packet. Have your grill hot and ready. Place the tomatoes on the grill. Close the lid and cook for 10 minutes or until the tomatoes are thoroughly heated. Remove the tomatoes from the grill and serve. Be careful when opening the packet as steam will escape and cause severe burns.

Fried Green Tomato Salad

Makes 6 servings

1/2 cup plain white or yellow cornmeal
1 tsp. dried mint
1 tsp. ground cumin
3/4 tsp. salt
1/2 cup buttermilk
3 large green tomatoes, cut into 1/4" thick slices
Vegetable oil for frying
2 large heads Bibb lettuce, torn into bite size pieces
1/2 cup toasted walnuts
3 shallots, finely chopped
1 tbs. honey
1/3 cup red wine vinegar
1/3 cup vegetable oil
3 tbs. walnut oil

In a mixing bowl, add the cornmeal, mint, cumin, salt and buttermilk. Whisk until well combined. Dip each tomato slice in the batter allowing the excess batter to drip off back into the bowl.

In a large skillet over medium high heat, add vegetable oil to a depth of 2" in the skillet. You will need to fry the tomatoes in batches. When the oil is sizzling hot, add the tomatoes. Fry about 3 minutes on each side or until the tomatoes are golden brown. Remove the tomatoes from the oil and drain on paper towels.

Place the lettuce on a serving platter. Place the tomatoes over the lettuce. Sprinkle the walnuts over the top. In a small bowl, add the shallots, honey, red wine vinegar, 1/3 cup vegetable oil and walnut oil. Whisk until the dressing is well combined. Drizzle the dressing to taste over the salad and serve.

BLT Layered Salad

Makes 8 servings

1 cup sour cream
1 cup mayonnaise
1 tbs. lemon juice
1 tsp. dried basil
1/2 tsp. salt
1/2 tsp. black pepper
4 cups iceberg lettuce, torn into bite size pieces
2 lbs. bacon, cooked crisp and crumbled
6 cups diced fresh tomatoes
3 cups large croutons

In a small bowl, add the sour cream, mayonnaise, lemon juice, basil, salt and black pepper. Stir until well combined. Place the lettuce in the bottom of a 9 x 13 baking dish. Sprinkle the bacon over the lettuce. Sprinkle the tomatoes over the bacon. Spread the sour cream dressing over the top of the salad. Be sure to cover every bit of the salad spreading the dressing all the way to the dish.

Cover the dish and chill at least 2 hours before serving. When ready to serve, remove the salad from the refrigerator. Remove the cover and sprinkle the croutons over the top.

Charred Tomato Salad

Makes 6 servings

8 large fresh tomatoes, seeded and quartered
1/2 cup plus 2 tbs. olive oil
1/3 cup sliced fresh basil
3 tbs. red wine vinegar
1 tsp. salt
1/2 tsp. black pepper

Pat the tomatoes dry with paper towels. Brush 2 tablespoons olive oil over the sides of the tomatoes. You will need to cook the tomatoes in batches. In a large cast iron skillet over high heat, add the tomatoes. Cook for 2 minutes on each side or until the tomatoes begin to turn black. Remove the skillet from the heat. Let the tomatoes cool completely in the skillet. Remove the tomatoes from the skillet and place in a large bowl. Leave the juice in the skillet.

Add 1/2 cup olive oil, basil, red wine vinegar, salt and black pepper to the skillet. Whisk until the dressing is well combined. Pour the dressing over the tomatoes. Toss until combined. Cover the bowl and let the salad sit at room temperature for 1 hour. Stir the tomatoes 3 times during the process. Remove the cover from the bowl and serve.

Tomato Bread Salad

Makes 8 servings

8 cups cubed Italian bread
4 cups chopped fresh tomatoes
1 cup minced fresh basil
1/2 cup thinly sliced purple onion
1/2 cup olive oil
2 tbs. red wine vinegar
1/2 tsp. salt
1/2 tsp. black pepper
1 garlic clove, minced

In a large serving bowl, add the bread, tomatoes, basil and purple onion. In a small bowl, add the olive oil, red wine vinegar, salt, black pepper and garlic. Whisk until the dressing is smooth and well combined. Pour the dressing over the salad. Toss until all the ingredients are combined.

Let the salad sit at room temperature for 30 minutes before serving. Toss the salad again before serving.

BLT Chicken Salad

Makes 8 servings

1/2 cup mayonnaise
3 tbs. barbecue sauce
2 tbs. finely chopped onion
1 tbs. fresh lemon juice
1/4 tsp. black pepper
8 cups lettuce, torn into bite size pieces
3 cups diced tomatoes
4 cups diced cooked chicken
10 bacon slices, cooked and crumbled
2 hard boiled eggs, sliced

In a small bowl, add the mayonnaise, barbecue sauce, onion, lemon juice and black pepper. Whisk until well combined. Cover the bowl and refrigerate at least 2 hours before serving.

When ready to serve, add the lettuce, tomatoes, chicken, bacon and eggs to a serving bowl. Spoon the dressing over the top and toss until all the ingredients are combined.

Southern Garden Tomato & Cucumber Salad

Makes 4 servings

2 cups chopped and seeded cucumbers
3 1/2 cups seeded and chopped fresh tomatoes
1/2 cup chopped green bell pepper
1/2 cup chopped purple onion
1/3 cup vegetable oil
3 tbs. granulated sugar
3 tbs. red wine vinegar
3/4 tsp. salt
1/8 tsp. black pepper

Add the cucumbers, tomatoes, green bell pepper and purple onion to a mixing bowl. In a small bowl, add the vegetable oil, granulated sugar, red wine vinegar, salt and black pepper. Whisk until the dressing is smooth and combined. Pour the dressing over the vegetables and toss until all the vegetables are coated in the dressing. Cover the salad and chill for 3 hours before serving.

Tomatoes with Fresh Peaches & Goat Cheese

Makes 6 servings

1/3 cup white balsamic vinegar
1 garlic clove, minced
2 tbs. light brown sugar
2 tbs. olive oil
1/8 tsp. salt
1 cup diced fresh peach
2 tbs. chopped fresh basil
4 cups sliced tomatoes, 1/2" thick
3 oz. goat cheese, crumbled
1/2 cup chopped toasted pecans
Black pepper to taste

In a mixing bowl, add the white balsamic vinegar, garlic, brown sugar, olive oil and salt. Whisk until all the ingredients are combined. Add the peach and basil to the bowl. Toss until the peach is coated in the dressing.

Place the tomato slices on a platter. Spoon the peach and dressing over the tomatoes. Sprinkle the goat cheese and pecans over the tomatoes. Season to taste with black pepper and serve.

Tomato Caper Salad

Makes 4 servings

2 tbs. balsamic vinegar
1 tbs. drained small capers
4 tsp. olive oil
1/2 tsp. black pepper
2 cups diced tomatoes
6 basil leaves, shredded
4 cups lettuce, torn into bite size pieces

In a mixing bowl, add the balsamic vinegar, capers, olive oil and black pepper. Whisk until well combined and add the tomatoes and basil. Toss until the tomatoes are coated in the dressing. Let the tomatoes sit for 30 minutes at room temperature.

Place the lettuce on a serving platter. Spoon the tomatoes and dressing over the lettuce and serve.

Feta Stuffed Tomatoes

Makes 8 servings

4 large tomatoes, halved horizontally
4 oz. crumbled feta cheese
1/4 cup fine dry breadcrumbs
2 tbs. chopped green onion
2 tbs. chopped fresh parsley
2 tbs. olive oil

Remove the pulp from the tomato halves and chop the pulp. Place the chopped pulp in a mixing bowl. Add the feta cheese, breadcrumbs, green onion, parsley and olive oil. Toss until all the ingredients are combined. Spoon the mixture into the tomato halves.

Preheat the oven to 350°. Place the tomatoes in a 9 x 13 baking pan. Bake for 15 minutes. Remove the tomatoes from the oven and serve.

Herb Stuffed Tomatoes

Makes 8 servings

1 cup chopped celery
1 cup chopped onion
1/2 cup unsalted butter
2 cups dry bread, cubed
1/4 cup minced fresh parsley
2 tsp. rubbed sage
1 tsp. dried thyme
1/2 tsp. salt
1/2 tsp. black pepper
1/4 cup chicken broth
8 fresh tomatoes

In a dutch oven over medium heat, add the celery, onion and butter. Saute the vegetables for 5 minutes. Add the bread cubes, parsley, sage, thyme, salt, black pepper and chicken broth. Stir until all the ingredients are combined. Remove the pan from the heat.

Cut a thin slice off the top of each tomato. Scoop out the pulp and seeds and discard. Place the tomatoes, upside down, on paper towels. Allow the tomatoes to drain for 10 minutes. Spray a 11 x 7 baking dish with non stick cooking spray. Place the tomatoes, right side up, in the baking dish. Fill the tomatoes with the stuffing.

Preheat the oven to 350°. Bake for 30 minutes. Remove the tomatoes from the oven and serve.

Tomato Mozzarella Saute

Makes 4 servings

1/4 cup chopped shallots
1 garlic clove, minced
1 tsp. minced fresh thyme
2 tsp. olive oil
2 1/2 cups cherry tomatoes, halved
1/4 tsp. salt
1/4 tsp. black pepper
4 oz. fresh mozzarella cheese, cut into 1/2" cubes

In a skillet over medium heat, add the shallots, garlic, thyme and olive oil. Saute the shallots about 4 minutes or until they are tender. Add the cherry tomatoes, salt and black pepper. Stir until combined. Cook only until the tomatoes are thoroughly heated. Remove the skillet from the heat.

Add the mozzarella cheese cubes and toss until combined. Serve hot.

Spinach Topped Tomatoes

Makes 6 servings

10 oz. pkg. frozen chopped spinach, thawed
2 chicken bouillon cubes
Salt to season
3 large tomatoes, halved
1 cup soft breadcrumbs
1/2 cup grated Parmesan cheese
1/2 cup chopped onion
1/2 cup melted unsalted butter
1 beaten egg
1 garlic clove, minced
1/4 tsp. black pepper
1/8 tsp. cayenne pepper
1/2 cup freshly shredded Parmesan cheese

In a sauce pan over medium heat, add the spinach and chicken bouillon cubes. Do not add water unless you do not have any liquid from the spinach. Stir frequently and cook for 5 minutes or until the spinach is tender. Remove the pan from the heat and drain all liquid from the spinach. Pat the spinach dry with paper towels to remove all the moisture.

Season the tomato halves with salt to taste. Place the tomatoes, upside down, on paper towels to drain. Drain the tomatoes for 15 minutes. In a mixing bowl, add the spinach, breadcrumbs, 1/2 cup grated Parmesan cheese, onion, butter, egg, garlic, black pepper and cayenne pepper. Stir until well combined.

Preheat the oven to 350°. Place the tomatoes, cut side up, in a baking dish. Spread the spinach mixture over the top of the tomatoes. Bake for 15 minutes or until the spinach and tomatoes are thoroughly heated. Remove the tomatoes from the oven and sprinkle 1/2 cup shredded Parmesan cheese over the top. Allow the tomatoes to cool for 5 minutes before serving.

Fresh Tomatoes in Vinaigrette

Makes 4 servings

6 tbs. white vinegar
6 tbs. vegetable oil
4 tbs. granulated sugar
2 tsp. season salt
4 tomatoes, cut into wedges

Add the white vinegar, vegetable oil, granulated sugar and season salt to a glass jar. Place the lid on the jar and shake until the vinaigrette is well combined. Place the tomato wedges on a serving platter. Pour the vinaigrette over the tomatoes and serve.

Broiled Feta Tomatoes

Makes 6 servings

6 fresh tomatoes
Salt and black pepper to season
1/2 tsp. dried Italian seasoning
1 cup crumbled feta cheese
1/4 cup bottled Italian dressing

Cut the tomatoes in half lengthwise. Place the tomatoes, cut side up, on a baking sheet. Sprinkle the salt and black pepper to taste over the tomatoes. Sprinkle the Italian seasoning and feta cheese over the tomatoes. Drizzle the Italian dressing over the tomatoes.

Preheat the oven to the broiler position. Broil for 2 minutes or until the feta cheese just begins to brown. Remove the tomatoes from the oven and cool for 2 minutes before serving.

Fresh Tomato Rice

This is delicious served with shrimp, fresh fish, chicken or pork.

Makes 4 servings

1 cup dry long grain rice
2 tsp. olive oil
1 tbs. tomato paste
2 cups water
2 cups chopped fresh tomato
Salt and black pepper to taste

In a sauce pan over medium heat, add the rice and olive oil. Saute the rice for 3 minutes or until the rice begins to brown. Add the tomato paste and water to the pan. Stir until well combined and bring the rice to a boil. When the rice is boiling, reduce the heat to low. Place a lid on the pan and simmer the rice for 15 minutes or until the rice is tender.

Add the tomatoes to the rice. Stir until combined and remove the pan from the heat. Allow the rice to sit undisturbed for 5 minutes. Season the rice to taste with salt and black pepper. Fluff the rice with a fork and serve.

BLT Pasta Salad

Makes 6 servings

1 1/4 cups dry pasta shells, hot and cooked
4 bacon slices, cooked and chopped
2 1/2 cups diced tomatoes
1/2 cup ranch salad dressing

Add all the ingredients to a serving bowl. Toss until all the ingredients are well combined. Cover the bowl and chill for 2 hours before serving.

Tomato Avocado Salad

Makes 6 servings

2 avocados, peeled and sliced
2 large tomatoes, cut into wedges
1 onion, cut into thin wedges
1 cup bottled Italian salad dressing

In a serving bowl, add the avocados, tomatoes and onion. Pour the Italian dressing over the salad. Gently toss until the dressing coats the vegetables. Chill the salad for 20 minutes before serving.

This salad is great by itself or spoon the leftovers over burgers and sandwiches.

Tomato Corn Salad

Makes 6 servings

3 large chopped tomatoes
1/2 cup diced purple onion
1/3 cup green onion
1/4 cup balsamic vinegar
3 tbs. minced fresh basil
1 tbs. minced fresh cilantro
1 tsp. salt
1/2 tsp. black pepper
4 cups fresh corn
3 garlic cloves, peeled and thinly sliced
2 tbs. olive oil
1 tbs. Dijon mustard

In a serving bowl, add the tomatoes, purple onion, green onion, balsamic vinegar, basil, cilantro, salt and black pepper. Toss until combined. In a skillet over medium heat, add the corn, garlic and olive oil. Saute the corn for 6 minutes or until the corn is tender. Remove the skillet from the heat and stir in the Dijon mustard. Add the corn to the vegetables in the bowl. Toss until combined and serve.

Italian Tomato Salad

Makes 6 servings

5 tbs. olive oil
1 1/2 tsp. red wine vinegar
2 tbs. minced fresh basil
1 tbs. minced fresh parsley
1 garlic clove, peeled
1/4 tsp. salt
1/8 tsp. black pepper
4 fresh tomatoes, sliced
1/2 cup thinly sliced purple onion

Separate the onion slices into rings. In a blender, add the olive oil, red wine vinegar, basil, parsley, garlic, salt and black pepper. Process until smooth and combined.

Place the tomatoes in a serving dish. Place the onion rings over the tomatoes. Pour the dressing over the tomatoes and onions before serving.

Tomato Zucchini Salad

Makes 8 servings

2 cups water
4 cups sliced zucchini
1/8 tsp. salt
2 tomatoes, cut into wedges
2 slices purple onion, separated into rings
3 tbs. olive oil
1 tbs. balsamic vinegar
1 tbs. minced fresh tarragon
1 tbs. Dijon mustard
1/2 tsp. salt
1/2 tsp. Tabasco sauce
1 garlic clove, minced
1 tbs. minced fresh parsley

In a sauce pan over medium heat, add the zucchini, 1/8 teaspoon salt and water. Bring the zucchini to a boil and cook for 3 minutes. Remove the pan from the heat and drain all the water from the zucchini. Rinse the zucchini in cold water until they are cool. Drain all the water from the zucchini and pat the zucchini dry with paper towels.

Add the zucchini, tomatoes and onion to a serving bowl. In a jar with a lid, add the olive oil, balsamic vinegar, tarragon, Dijon mustard, 1/2 teaspoon salt, Tabasco sauce and garlic. Place the lid on the jar and shake until all the ingredients are combined. Pour the dressing over the salad. Toss until all the ingredients are combined. Sprinkle the parsley over the top and serve.

Cilantro Lime Marinated Tomatoes

Makes 6 servings

6 tomatoes, cut into wedges
3 tbs. olive oil
2 tbs. fresh lime juice
1 tbs. chopped fresh cilantro
1/2 tsp. garlic salt
1/4 tsp. grated lime zest
1/8 tsp. black pepper

Place the tomatoes in a shallow dish. In a small bowl, add the olive oil, lime juice, cilantro, garlic salt, lime zest and black pepper. Stir until combined and pour over the tomatoes. Toss the tomatoes until they are coated in the marinade. Cover the dish and chill for 1 hour before serving.

Basil and Balsamic Marinated Tomatoes

Makes 12 servings

1 cup thinly sliced purple onion
4 cups ice water
3/4 cup balsamic vinegar
1/4 cup olive oil
2 tbs. water
2 tsp. granulated sugar
1/2 tsp. salt
1/2 tsp. black pepper
2 garlic cloves, minced
1/2 cup chopped fresh basil
6 tomatoes, thinly sliced
1 cup shredded Parmesan cheese
2 cups garlic croutons

Place the onion slices and 4 cups ice water in a mixing bowl. Soak the onions at room temperature for 30 minutes. Drain all the water from the onions. Pat the onions dry with paper towels.

In a mixing bowl, add the balsamic vinegar, olive oil, 2 tablespoons water, granulated sugar, salt, black pepper and garlic. Stir until well combined. Add the basil and stir until combined.

Place half the tomatoes in a shallow 2 quart baking dish. Place half the onion slices over the tomatoes. Pour half the dressing over the tomatoes. Repeat the layering process one more time. Cover the dish and chill for 30 minutes before serving.

When ready to serve, sprinkle the Parmesan cheese and croutons over the top of the salad.

Parsley Tomatoes

Makes 8 servings

8 tomatoes
1/4 cup olive oil
1/4 cup minced fresh parsley
2 tbs. cider vinegar
2 tsp. Dijon mustard
1 garlic clove, minced
1 tsp. salt
1 tsp. granulated sugar
1/4 tsp. black pepper

Cut a thin slice off the bottom of each tomato so the tomato sits flat. Cut each tomato into 1/2" slices. Place the tomato slices in a 9 x 13 baking dish. In a jar with a lid, add the olive oil, parsley, cider vinegar, Dijon mustard, garlic, salt, granulated sugar and black pepper. Place the lid on the jar and shake until combined. Pour the dressing over the tomatoes.

Cover the baking dish and refrigerate at least 4 hours before serving. Remove the tomatoes from the refrigerator 15 minutes before serving.

Tomato & Purple Onion Salad

Makes 4 servings

5 tomatoes, thinly sliced
1 cup purple onion, sliced and separated into rings
1/4 cup fresh lime juice
2 tbs. olive oil
1/2 tsp. granulated sugar
1/4 tsp. salt
1/4 cup minced fresh cilantro

Layer the tomatoes and purple onion in a serving bowl. In a jar with a lid, add the lime juice, olive oil, granulated sugar, salt and cilantro. Place the lid on the jar and shake until all the ingredients are combined. Pour the dressing over the tomatoes and onion. Toss to coat the tomato and onion in the dressing. Serve immediately.

Vidalia Onion Tomato Salad

Makes 6 servings

3 tbs. red wine vinegar
1 tbs. olive oil
1/2 tsp. granulated sugar
1/2 tsp. salt
1/2 tsp. yellow prepared mustard
1/4 tsp. black pepper
2 cups thinly sliced Vidalia onions
2 large tomatoes, cut into thin wedges
1/2 cup fresh basil, sliced
Salt and black pepper to taste

In a serving bowl, add the red wine vinegar, olive oil, granulated sugar, salt, mustard and black pepper. Whisk until well combined. Add the onions and toss until the onions are coated in the dressing. Cover the bowl and chill for 8 hours.

Add the tomatoes and basil to the salad. Season to taste with salt and black pepper. Toss until the tomatoes are coated in the dressing and serve.

Cucumber & Tomato Salad

Makes 8 servings

2 cucumbers, thinly sliced
4 green onions, thinly sliced
2 tbs. minced fresh parsley
1/4 cup sour cream
2 tbs. minced fresh dill
1 tbs. cider vinegar
1/2 tsp. salt
1/4 tsp. yellow prepared mustard
1/8 tsp. black pepper
2 tomatoes, thinly sliced

In a serving bowl, add the cucumbers, green onions, parsley, sour cream, dill, cider vinegar, salt, mustard and black pepper. Toss until all the ingredients are combined. Place the tomato slices over the top and serve.

Tomato Feta Salad

Makes 4 servings

1/4 cup bottled Greek dressing
2 tbs. chopped fresh parsley
2 1/2 cups chopped tomatoes
1/2 cup black olives
1/4 cup chopped purple onion
4 oz. pkg. feta cheese, sliced

In a serving bowl, add the Greek dressing, parsley, tomatoes, black olives and purple onion. Toss until all the ingredients are combined. Stir in the feta cheese. Cover the bowl and chill for 1 hour before serving.

To serve, drain all the liquid from the salad and serve as is or over lettuce.

Tomatoes with Horseradish Sauce

Makes 4 servings

1 tsp. unsalted butter
4 large tomatoes, sliced
3 tbs. mayonnaise
2 tbs. half and half
1 tbs. prepared horseradish
2 tbs. minced fresh parsley

In a large skillet over medium heat, add the butter. When the butter melts, add the tomato slices. Cook for 2 minutes on each side or until the tomatoes begin to brown. Remove the skillet from the heat.

In a small bowl, add the mayonnaise, half and half and horseradish. Stir until combined and spoon over the tomatoes. Sprinkle the parsley over the top and serve.

Roasted Tomato & Pepper Salad

Makes 6 servings

3 large fresh tomatoes, cut into 1/2" slices
1 yellow bell pepper, seeded and halved
1 green bell pepper, seeded and halved
1 red bell pepper, seeded and halved
1 purple onion, cut into 8 wedges
1 tbs. olive oil
1 tbs. balsamic vinegar
1 garlic clove, minced
1/2 tsp. salt
1/2 tsp. dried oregano
1/2 tsp. black pepper
1/4 cup sliced fresh basil

Line a baking sheet with aluminum foil. Spray the aluminum foil with non stick cooking spray. Preheat the oven to the broiler position. Place the tomatoes on the baking sheet. Broil the tomatoes for 4 minutes on each side or until they are slightly roasted. Remove the tomatoes from the oven but leave the broiler on.

Line a baking sheet with aluminum foil. Spray the aluminum foil with non stick cooking spray. Place the red, green and yellow peppers, cut side down, on the baking sheet. Place the onion wedges on the baking sheet. Broil the peppers and onions for 8 minutes on each side or until they are charred and blistered. Remove the peppers from the oven and immediately place the peppers in a Ziploc bag. Close the bag and let the peppers sit for 10 minutes. Leave the onions sitting on the baking sheet while the peppers rest. Remove the peppers from the bag and remove the charred skin. Cut the peppers into thin strips.

Add the tomatoes, onion and peppers to a mixing bowl. In a small bowl, add the olive oil, balsamic vinegar, garlic, salt, oregano and black pepper. Whisk until the dressing is smooth and combined. Pour the dressing over the vegetables. Toss until the vegetables are coated in the dressing. Sprinkle the basil over the top and serve.

Tomato & Tortilla Chip Salad

Makes 6 servings

8 cups lettuce, torn into bite size pieces
3 cups chopped tomato
15 oz. can dark red kidney beans, drained and rinsed
2 cups shredded cheddar cheese
1 cup crushed tortilla chips
1/2 cup cider vinegar
1/2 cup vegetable oil
1 envelope dry Italian dressing mix

Place the lettuce in a large serving bowl. Spoon the tomatoes over the lettuce. Spoon the kidney beans over the tomatoes. Sprinkle the cheddar cheese and tortilla chips over the beans.

In a jar with a lid, add the cider vinegar, vegetable oil and Italian dressing mix. Place a lid on the jar and shake until the dressing is combined. Drizzle the dressing over the top of the salad before serving.

Spicy Tomato Salad

Makes 5 cups

4 yellow banana peppers, seeded and diced
2 green banana peppers, seeded and diced
2 jalapeno peppers, seeded and diced
5 large tomatoes, seeded and diced
2 garlic cloves, minced
1 tbs. chopped fresh basil
1 tbs. chopped fresh parsley
1 tsp. chopped fresh rosemary
1 tsp. chopped fresh oregano
2 oz. cheddar cheese, cubed
1/2 cup olive oil
1 tbs. fresh lemon juice
1 tsp. salt
1/2 tsp. black pepper

In a serving bowl, add the green and yellow banana peppers, jalapeno peppers, tomatoes, garlic, basil, parsley, rosemary, oregano and cheddar cheese. In a jar with a lid, add the olive oil, lemon juice, salt and black pepper. Place a lid on the jar and shake until all the ingredients are combined. Pour the dressing over the peppers and tomatoes. Toss until all the ingredients are combined.

Cover the bowl and chill at least 2 hours but not more than 4 hours. Drain all the liquid from the salad and serve.

5 SOUPS

Tomato soup is most commonly known for the canned soup. Start with fresh tomatoes and the recipes will give you a new take on tomato soup.

Chunky Tomato Fruit Gazpacho

Makes 9 cups

2 cups finely diced cantaloupe
2 cups finely diced honeydew melon
2 cups finely diced fresh tomatoes
1 mango, finely diced
2 cups cucumbers, seeded and finely diced
1 jalapeno pepper, seeded and minced
1 cup finely diced fresh peaches
2 cups fresh orange juice
1/2 cup finely chopped onion
1/4 cup chopped fresh basil
3 tbs. chopped fresh mint
3 tbs. fresh lemon juice
1 tsp. granulated sugar
1/2 tsp. salt

Add all the ingredients to a serving bowl. Toss until all the ingredients are combined. Cover the bowl and chill at least 12 hours but no more than 24 hours before serving.

Yellow Tomato Gazpacho

Makes 2 quarts

3 yellow tomatoes, seeded and chopped
1 yellow bell pepper, seeded and chopped
1 cucumber, peeled, seeded and chopped
1 garlic clove, chopped
3 peaches, peeled and chopped
1/2 cup chopped Vidalia onion
1/4 cup lime juice
2 tbs. rice wine vinegar
1 tbs. Worcestershire sauce
1/2 tsp. Tabasco sauce
1 1/2 tsp. salt
1/2 tsp. black pepper

Add the tomatoes, yellow bell pepper, cucumber, garlic, peaches and onion to a blender. Process until smooth and combined. Pour the puree into a serving bowl.

Add the lime juice, rice wine vinegar, Worcestershire sauce, Tabasco sauce, salt and black pepper. Stir until all the ingredients are combined. Cover the bowl and chill for 4 hours before serving.

Tomato Corn Chowder

Makes 8 servings

4 bacon slices, diced
1 1/4 cups chopped onion
4 cups whole kernel corn
4 cups diced tomatoes
1 cup tomato juice
4 potatoes, peeled and diced

In a large sauce pan over medium heat, add the bacon. Cook for 6 minutes or until the bacon is crispy. Remove the bacon from the skillet and drain on paper towels. Drain all but 1 tablespoon bacon drippings from the pan.

Add the onion to the pan. Saute the onion for 5 minutes. Add the corn, tomatoes, tomato juice and potatoes to the pan. Stir frequently and cook for 25 minutes or until the potatoes are tender. Remove the pan from the heat. Crumble the bacon and sprinkle the bacon over the top before serving.

Brie Tomato Soup

Makes 6 servings

1/2 cup diced onion
2 tbs. olive oil
3 garlic cloves, minced
7 cups diced tomatoes
1 3/4 cups chicken broth
5 oz. pkg. Brie cheese, rind removed
1 tsp. salt
1/2 tsp. black pepper
2 cups croutons (use your favorite flavor)

In a dutch oven over medium heat, add the onion and olive oil. Saute the onion for 8 minutes. Add the garlic and saute the garlic for 1 minute. Add the tomatoes and chicken broth to the pan. Stir constantly and bring the soup to a boil. Stir frequently and cook for 10 minutes. Remove the soup from the heat and cool for 10 minutes.

Cut the Brie cheese into small pieces. Add the Brie to the soup. Stir until the cheese melts. Pour the soup into a large blender. Process until the soup is smooth and combined.

Pour the soup back into the pan. Place the pan over medium heat. Stir constantly and cook only until the soup is thoroughly heated. Do not let the soup boil. Stir in the salt and black pepper. Remove the pan from the heat and spoon the soup into bowls. Sprinkle the croutons over the top and serve.

Beefy Tomato Rice Soup

Makes 8 cups

1 lb. beef roast, thinly sliced
2 tbs. olive oil
1 cup chopped celery
2 1/2 cups chopped onion
2 garlic cloves, minced
1 tbs. dried Italian seasoning
5 1/4 cups beef broth
6 oz. pkg. wild rice, rinsed
2 1/2 cups diced tomatoes
1 cup sliced fresh mushrooms
1/4 tsp. Tabasco sauce
1 tsp. salt
1 tsp. black pepper
1 bay leaf

In a large dutch oven over medium heat, add the olive oil. When the oil is hot, add the beef. Stir constantly and cook the beef for 3 minutes or until the beef is well browned.

Add the celery, onion, garlic and Italian seasoning. Saute the vegetables for 5 minutes. Add the rice, beef broth, tomatoes, mushrooms, Tabasco sauce, salt, black pepper and bay leaf. Stir until all the ingredients are well combined. Bring the soup to a boil. When the soup is boiling, reduce the heat to low. Stir occasionally and simmer the soup for 30 minutes.

Place a lid on the pan and simmer the soup for 30 minutes or until the rice is tender. Remove the pan from the heat. Remove the bay leaf and discard.

Roasted Garlic and Basil Tomato Soup

Makes 4 servings

6 large garlic cloves, peeled
8 shallots, peeled and halved
2 tbs. olive oil
4 cups diced fresh tomatoes
3 cups chicken broth
1 tsp. Tabasco sauce
1 tsp. balsamic vinegar
1/2 tsp. salt
1/4 tsp. black pepper
1/8 tsp. cayenne pepper
3 tbs. minced fresh basil

Line an 8" baking pan with aluminum foil. Place the garlic cloves and shallots in the pan. Drizzle the olive oil over the garlic and shallots. Preheat the oven to 450°. Bake for 20 minutes or until the garlic and shallots are tender. Remove the pan from the oven and cool completely.

Add the garlic, shallots, tomatoes, 1 1/2 cups chicken broth, Tabasco sauce, balsamic vinegar, salt, black pepper and cayenne pepper to a blender. Process until the soup is smooth and combined. Pour the mixture into a sauce pan.

Place the pan over medium heat and add the remaining 1 1/2 cups chicken broth. Stir until well combined and bring the soup to a boil. Remove the pan from the heat and stir in the basil. Serve immediately.

Fresh Tomato Soup

Makes 1 quart

4 cups finely chopped tomatoes
1/2 tsp. baking soda
2 cups whole milk
2 tbs. unsalted butter

In a sauce pan over medium heat, add the tomatoes. Stir constantly and bring the tomatoes to a boil. Cook for 5 minutes. Mash the tomatoes with a potato masher until they are slightly chunky. Remove the pan from the heat.

Add the baking soda, milk and butter to the pan. Place the pan back on the heat and cook until the butter melts and the soup is thoroughly heated. Do not let the soup boil once you add the milk. Remove the pan from the heat and serve.

This is very good with sandwiches, salads or by itself as a light lunch or snack.

Tomato Dill Soup

Makes 4 servings

1 cup thinly sliced onion
1 garlic clove, minced
2 tbs. vegetable oil
1 tbs. unsalted butter
3 large tomatoes, sliced
1/2 tsp. salt
1/8 tsp. black pepper
6 oz. can tomato paste
1/4 cup all purpose flour
2 cups water
3/4 cup heavy whipping cream, whipped
1 tsp. dried dill

In a large sauce pan over medium heat, add the onion, garlic, vegetable oil and butter. Saute the onion and garlic for 6 minutes or until the onion is tender. Add the tomatoes, salt and black pepper to the pan. Stir constantly and cook until the soup is thoroughly heated. Remove the pan from the heat and stir in the tomato paste.

In a small bowl, add the all purpose flour and water. Whisk until well combined and add to the soup. Stir until all the ingredients are combined. Place the pan over medium heat. Stir constantly and bring the soup to a boil. Boil the soup for 2 minutes. Remove the pan from the heat.

Add the soup to a blender and process until smooth. Add the whipping cream and dill to the soup. Stir until combined and serve.

Chunky Tomato Basil Bisque

Makes 5 servings

6 celery ribs, chopped
1 1/2 cups chopped onion
1 red bell pepper, chopped
1/4 cup unsalted butter, cubed
7 cups chopped fresh tomatoes
1 tbs. tomato paste
3/4 cup basil leaves, chopped
3 tsp. granulated sugar
2 tsp. salt
1/2 tsp. black pepper
1 1/2 cups heavy whipping cream

In a large sauce pan over medium heat, add the celery, onion, red bell pepper, butter and tomatoes. Stir constantly and cook for 10 minutes. The vegetables should be tender when ready.

Add the tomato paste to the pan. Stir until combined and bring the soup to a boil. When the soup is boiling, reduce the heat to low. Stir occasionally and simmer the soup for 30 minutes. Remove the pan from the heat and stir in the basil, granulated sugar, salt, black pepper and whipping cream. Serve hot.

Mushroom Tomato Bisque

Makes 4 servings

6 cups halved tomatoes
5 tbs. olive oil
2 garlic cloves, minced
1/2 tsp. salt
1/2 tsp. dried basil
1/2 tsp. dried oregano
1/2 tsp. black pepper
3 cups sliced fresh mushrooms
1/2 cup finely chopped onion
1 1/4 cups chicken broth
1/3 cup tomato paste
3/4 cup heavy whipping cream
2 tbs. grated Parmesan cheese

Spray a 15 x 10 x 1 baking pan with non stick cooking spray. Place the tomatoes, cut side down, on the baking pan. Brush 3 tablespoons olive oil over the tomatoes. In a small bowl, add the garlic, salt, basil, oregano and black pepper. Stir until combined and sprinkle over the tomatoes.

Preheat the oven to 450°. Bake for 20 minutes or until the tomatoes begin to brown. Remove the pan from the oven. Cool the tomatoes for 10 minutes. Add the tomatoes and any pan drippings to a blender. Process until the tomatoes are smooth and combined.

In a large sauce pan over medium heat, add 2 tablespoons olive oil, mushrooms and onion. Saute the mushrooms for 8 minutes or until they are tender. Stir in the chicken broth and tomato paste. Stir until well combined and bring the soup to a boil. Once the soup is boiling, remove the pan from the heat.

Stir in the tomato puree, heavy whipping cream and Parmesan cheese. Serve immediately.

CHAPTER INDEX

Appetizers, Sauces & Spreads

Main Dishes & Casseroles

Tomato Onion Pie, 26
Tomato Bacon Pie, 27
Beefy Tomato Pie, 28
Tomato Quiche, 29
Tomato Spinach Quiche, 30
Tomato & Cheese Omelet, 31
Rustic Tomato Tart, 32
Tuscan Spinach & Tomato Tart, 33
Tomato Vegetable Gratin, 34
BLT Tomato Basil Tart, 35
Fontina Tomato Tart, 36
Tomato Leek & Bacon Tart, 37
Tomato Bacon Strata, 38
Steak with Tomato Onion Relish, 39
Tomato Shrimp Creole Skillet, 40
Mediterranean Chicken, 41
Stuffed Fried Green Tomato Casserole, 42
Tomato Topped Halibut, 44
Grilled Meatless Margherita Pizzas, 45
Grilled Tomato Pizza, 46
Fresh Tomato Fettuccine, 47
Tomato Eggplant Bake, 48
Tomato Onion Salmon, 49
Sausage Tomato Pasta Skillet, 50
Tomato & Parmesan Gnocchi, 51
Fresh Tomato Prosciutto Penne, 52
Fresh Tomato Mushroom Pasta, 53
Greek Tomato Sauce with Penne, 54
Red Wine Tomato Pasta, 55
Spicy Tomato Vermicelli, 56
Fresh Tomato Linguine, 57
Grilled Tomato Feta Chicken, 58
Green Tomato Gumbo, 59
Great Northern Beans with Tomatoes, 60

Breads & Sandwiches

Side Dishes & Salads

Fried Green Tomatoes, 77
Herb Tomatoes & Green Beans, 78
Tomato Grits, 79
Spicy Tomato Macaroni & Cheese Skillet, 80
Roasted Rosemary Cherry Tomatoes, 81
Basil Cherry Tomatoes, 81
Cheesy Tomato Casserole, 82
Baked Green Tomatoes, 82
Creole Tomatoes & Hominy, 83
Fresh Tomato Pasta, 84
Tomato Spinach Saute, 85
Southern Fried Okra & Green Tomatoes, 86
Pan Fried Okra & Tomatoes, 87
Cheesy Baked Okra Tomato Casserole, 88
Grilled Tomatoes, 89
Fried Green Tomato Salad, 90
BLT Layered Salad, 91
Charred Tomato Salad, 92
Tomato Bread Salad, 93
BLT Chicken Salad, 94
Southern Garden Tomato & Cucumber Salad, 95
Tomatoes with Fresh Peaches & Goat Cheese, 96
Tomato Caper Salad, 97
Feta Stuffed Tomatoes, 98
Herb Stuffed Tomatoes, 99
Tomato Mozzarella Saute, 100
Spinach Topped Tomatoes, 101
Fresh Tomatoes in Vinaigrette, 102
Broiled Feta Tomatoes, 102
Fresh Tomato Rice, 103
BLT Pasta Salad, 104
Tomato Avocado Salad, 104
Tomato Corn Salad, 105
Italian Tomato Salad, 106
Tomato Zucchini Salad, 107
Cilantro Lime Marinated Tomatoes, 108
Basil and Balsamic Marinated Tomatoes, 109
Parsley Tomatoes, 110
Tomato & Purple Onion Salad, 111

Side Dishes & Salads cont'd

Vidalia Onion Tomato Salad, 112
Cucumber & Tomato Salad, 113
Tomato Feta Salad, 113
Tomatoes with Horseradish Sauce, 114
Roasted Tomato & Pepper Salad, 115
Tomato & Tortilla Chip Salad, 116
Spicy Tomato Salad, 117

Soups

Chunky Tomato Fruit Gazpacho, 119
Yellow Tomato Gazpacho, 120
Tomato Corn Chowder, 121
Brie Tomato Soup, 122
Beefy Tomato Rice Soup, 123
Roasted Garlic and Basil Tomato Soup, 124
Fresh Tomato Soup, 125
Tomato Dill Soup, 126
Chunky Tomato Basil Bisque, 127
Mushroom Tomato Bisque, 128

ABOUT THE AUTHOR

Lifelong southerner who lives in Bowling Green, KY. Priorities in life are God, family and pets. I love to cook, garden and feed most any stray animal that walks into my yard. I love old cookbooks and cookie jars. Huge NBA fan who loves to spend hours watching basketball games. Enjoy cooking for family and friends and hosting parties and reunions. Can't wait each year to build gingerbread houses for the kids.

Made in the USA
Monee, IL
12 August 2021

75581393R00083